Praise for Meg Losey's Work

For *Parenting the Children*

"Every parents and grandpar ... ve never come across anything quite lik

—P.M.H. Atwater, LHD, auth ... *nd the Indigo Children,*
The Big Book of Near-Death ...periences, and *Future Memory*

"This book is a wonderful guide to help parents nurture their children's gifts and deepest talents by mining the treasures of The Now."

—Judith Orloff, MD, author of *Second Sight*

"This book is required reading for parents raising any bright, aware, and sensitive child."

—Michael J Tamura, award-winning author of *You Are The Answer: Discovering and Fulfilling Your Soul's Purpose*

Praise for *Touching the Light*

"*Touching the Light* is the must have book for understanding home, health, and healing."

—Dannion Brinkley, *New York Times* bestseller author of *Saved by the Light* and *Secrets of the Light*

"This is a must read for everyone, and especially for those who are looking for alternatives to the confines of conventional medicine and Big Pharma."

—Bob Frissell, Flower of Life facilitator and author of *Nothing In This Book Is True, But It's Exactly How Things Are*

"As a practicing gyn-oncologist, I have observed that western medicine cannot explain the phenomena of placebo effects and spontaneous remissions. It virtually ignores a host of potentially useful therapies such as homeopathy and energy medicine that do not fit its paradigm of cause and effect. With her unique ability to communicate with her non-ascended Masters, Dr. Blackburn-Losey has written the definitive comprehensive text that explains these phenomena at a level of understanding not yet known to the majority of humanity. I highly recommend this book as required reading to all those interested in the evolution of integrative medicine."

—Matthew Burrell, MD

Praise for *The Secret History of Consciousness*

"Dr. Meg Blackburn Losey shows us how we can step out of the illusion of separation and into the greater truth of our multi-dimensional existence and our intimate connection to all life everywhere. The veils are lifting, and as we take back our creative powers we have an opportunity to completely redefine what it means to be human! This book speaks to that possibility."

—Bob Frissell, Flower of Life facilitator and author of
*Nothing In This Book Is True,
But It's Exactly How Things Are*

"*The Secret History of Consciousness* is a brilliant reflection of her personal experience into the dimensional worlds of human consciousness and potential. Only from this source does a book of this nature have any authority in the world."

—Drunvalo Melchizedek, founder of the
Flower of Life Workshops,
consultant for the Spirit of Ma'at,
and author of *The Serpent of Light*

The Art of Living Out Loud

The Art of Living Out Loud

how to leave behind your baggage and pain to
become a happy, whole, perfect human being
with unlimited potential

MEG BLACKBURN LOSEY, PHD

WEISERBOOKS
San Francisco, CA / Newburyport, MA

First published in 2012 by Weiser Books
Red Wheel/Weiser, LLC
With offices at:
665 Third Street, Suite 400
San Francisco, CA 94107
www.redwheelweiser.com

Illustrations by Meg Blackburn Losey, PhD.

ISBN: 978-1-57863-532-0

Library of Congress Cataloging-in-Publication data available upon request

Cover design by Jim Warner
Interior design by Jane Hagaman

Printed in the United States of America
MAL
10 9 8 7 6 5 4 3 2 1

The paper used in this publication meets the minimum requirements of the American National Standard for Information Sciences—Permanence of Paper for Printed Library Materials Z39.48-1992 (R1997).

To Travis

With all my heart

Life has no meaning if it is not truly lived. How we live is a choice. If we don't like the way things are going we can choose again. And again. And again. The choosing is important but what drives the choosing has everything to do with the outcome. What is vital is that we are willing to be honest with ourselves and change what we must so that we really know where we are going.

Contents

Acknowledgments

I couldn't have written this book from my singular human perspective. To each of you who, over the years, has confided in me, trusted me, and shared your life, your love, your grief, and even the depths of your pain, this book is a tribute to what we have learned together.

Note to Readers

This book is intended to be an informational guide and is not meant to treat, diagnose, or replace the professional guidance of counselors or health professionals. Always consult with a qualified specialist for serious concerns. Neither the author nor the publisher accepts any responsibility for your health or how you choose to use the information contained in this book.

Introduction

So here is the question: <u>Who are you and what do you want?</u>
I mean really. Most of us go about our lives with an idealistic
vision of what our lives should look like, what our experiences
should be, and yet most of us don't have a clue why our lives
aren't turning out the way we expected or planned.

If we ask ourselves who we really are and what it is we truly
want, most of us can't answer that question honestly or directly.
This is because we are trying to fit into other people's molds:
their expectations and ideals. Plus, we are conditioned from
birth to realize that we are not perfect—that we must achieve a
singular purpose in our lives and we have to do it all by a certain set of rules. So we flounder day after day with our dreams
just outside our grasp, our insecurities and fears leading the
way to certain and ultimate disaster. Believe me. I found out the
hard way what it means to struggle through life trying to please
everyone but myself.

Over ten years ago I found myself in what a lot of people
might call a dark night of the soul. I awoke on my friend's couch
sobbing. To this day I don't know what I was crying about.
Had I dreamed? Who knows? It could have been any number
of things that morning. Everything I had perceived to be my life
had fallen apart in a short two weeks. Life, Love, Work—all
gone in a flash. I had opted for my friend's couch because home
had become impossible. I was working out of my car because

my partners had literally pushed me out of the very business I had conceived, planned, and created. There was more, but suffice it to say that there was nothing left of life as I had known it.

As I lay curled up in a puddle of my tears, I knew something was terribly wrong. I knew that if I was to survive all the challenges now looming before me, I really needed to understand where I had gone wrong. As I took an honest look at my life and the relationships I had developed with others, there came a moment when I realized my life had been one lie after another. Lies I had accepted from others because I wanted something from them, lies I had told myself.

I realized that all of my successes had been one great big illusion, that they were successes based on the values of others—not mine.

I also realized I had no idea who I was or what I really wanted. So I began to consider each situation from the perspective of *me*. Not what anyone else said or did; my part of the play. My game. What was my part in all of this? What was I fighting so hard to save or to be? Given that I think of myself as a loving and gentle person, why was there so much conflict around me when my heart in truth wanted to experience life to its fullest potential? Conflict was the last thing I wanted. All I ever wanted was to be loved and accepted, but somehow it felt as though I was surrounded by sharks and I was the only one on the menu! Why was it so hard? What was my part in this disaster I called my life?

As I considered all of these things and more, I began to realize that the life I had created was based upon what I thought everyone else wanted me to be. I was trying to be the star of someone else's play. What did I want? I had no idea. Who was I, really? Who knew? I was a lie to myself.

One thing I realized beyond a shadow of a doubt that fateful morning was that enough was enough. I got it. I really got it. I was done. No more lies, no more self-deception, no more trying to be what everyone else expected. I looked up and said to no one in particular, "Whoever I am, whatever this is, I accept!"

They say you get what you ask for, but I had no idea how true that could be. That morning was the beginning of a life that is pure magic. As humble as I was, as low as I had fallen, the only way to go was up. No more being a victim of my own doing.

The first thing that happened was that the difficulties began to melt away. I lost weight. My body began to reflect who I really was. The people with whom I had been involved slunk into my past and others began to show up. Honest people. People who were open to the possibilities of greater reality. Positive people who lived from their hearts and interacted with sincerity and without self-agenda. They didn't want anything in particular from me, for them. They just wanted me as I am.

Each day, I practiced telling the truth to myself and others. Honestly, at first that was one of the scariest things I had ever done. I felt raw and exposed, but my conviction to be nothing less than the true me won time after time, day after day, and ultimately telling the truth became easier.

As I learned to be authentic, my intuitive gifts unfolded as precious realizations that there was much, much more to being alive than I had ever imagined. I began to realize the power of the moment and, even more important, of myself. I realized that life isn't so hard once you get the hang of it, but we have to live it from a set of very simple instructions. I learned that creating the kind of experience I wanted in life was as easy as believing it, and that worrying was nothing more than fear of "what-ifs," which didn't even exist.

I began to unfold, a beautiful human being who had no stories to cover up, no lies to tell—just an authentic being on a mission to myself. As each day became easier, my days also became more magical, and I realized I was on to something.

I was not just at ease, I was free. I was present with myself, truly in the now, for the first time in my life, and I actually liked me. My intuitive gifts became vast. It seemed that there was no end to the realities I could create from my new life perspective. All I had to do was think something and it became instant reality. If there was something I wanted to know or understand, someone I had never met before showed up in my living room with the answers. It seemed that every single time I had information that was far beyond my frame of reference, somehow the person who could understand it best and even help me put the information to use would hear about me and either show up at my door or make an appointment for a session with me. Talk about synchronicities; I became the queen of them! I learned to laugh at myself, learned to express my inner passions, emotions, even my fears. The little kid in me was no longer afraid to come out and play. People began to notice great changes in me and wanted to know what I was doing. I tried to tell them but the concept of self-honesty was so new to me that I didn't really have words. Sometimes there just aren't any.

As my new life unfolded, one day a man came to my home and asked me to speak at a weekend conference. Since our community was fairly small, word got around quickly . . . about everything, and particularly about me. I had become the local mystery and excitement. Before that moment I hadn't even considered such an idea. I was at once elated and terrified. Who would believe me? Why would anyone want to hear my experiences? And yet something deep inside of me screamed at me to share what I had learned, so I agreed. The weekend of the expo I showed up and shuffled my feet while I told my story. I really thought everyone would leave. I was far from right. That lecture was the beginning of an entirely new and different life path for me. Not only did no one walk out on me that day, when my allotted time was over, no one moved. They were riveted in their seats, wanting more. Wow. Wow.

That weekend I met numerous people, and each became an important facet of my life. I grew to love every one of them dearly. It was as if a family of souls had traveled forever and come to rest in one place in one moment in time. Some became business associates over time, and some became great friends. I even met my husband there.

Since that fateful weekend, I have continued to follow each synchronicity that comes my way without a thought or concern. I have learned a new definition of Faith. I have learned the true meaning of letting go. And I have learned to love myself.

For over fifteen years now I have worked with individuals and groups in the capacity of healer, counselor, teacher, and spiritual advisor. I have traveled around the world as a spirit guide, lecturer, keynote speaker, and instructor, teaching countless people how to create the kind of lives *they* want.

Throughout this time, no matter where I was or who was in the audience, the same issues came up over and over again. Nearly everyone had the same burning questions, all of them ones that I had faced in my own quest for a greater life.

As I listened to these commonly related, repetitive issues I read between the lines. As I did, I felt a great need in people for more than our world seems to offer. Something was missing. And yet, while so many seek answers outside themselves, I realized that everything we need is right here inside of us. To me, who we are or what we are capable of has nothing to do with any particular belief system. The real secret is that there is no secret. We already have everything we need to be, have, or experience whatever we want. There is magic inside each and every one of us. We can create anything we want anywhere, any time; we need only the right set of tools and the realization that we are subject to no one else's ideas, or ideals, but our own.

I want to share these tools with you. You have gifts and abilities that you haven't even considered. Why not discover who you really are and what you really want and begin to create your life intentionally, creating from moment to moment the very kind of life that you want?

It is time to stop stumbling through life; I call this living by accident. We have the power. The bottom line is that life is a choice. My question to you, the reader, is: Who is doing your choosing?

The Art of Living Out Loud is about finding your power from the inside out. It is about taking that power into the creative process of your very life to find yourself fulfilled and overflowing with abundance. This book is about how, when we drop our pretenses and our perceptions of control, shed our fears, and embrace who we are, our creative gifts not only blossom, we can create a perfect life right here on earth.

Life is a series of choices, moment to moment. In each of those moments are signposts, clues, and even synchronicities that bring us closer to our intended goals. If we are living in fear, if we are bound by uncertainties, if we are worried about what has already happened or what is next, we are missing the boat. *The Art of Living Out Loud* will literally teach you how to shed those fears, uncertainties, and perceptions of being less than and bring you clearly onto a path of universal co-creation.

This is a new Beginning for you. It is an opportunity for you to change your consciousness from never ending questions to a totality of answers.

The Art of Living Out Loud will bring you not only self-empowerment, but empowerment in everyday life. This is not just a book of self-help advice. *The Art of Living Out Loud* is a book with an attitude. In it, you will find no-nonsense truth that may hit you square between the eyes or in the heart. So be it. We can indefinitely or forever skirt around our issues or we can quit deluding ourselves and get to it. *The Art of Living Out Loud* is a journey through self, an embracing of the infinite possibilities that are available to us as human beings and infinite souls. This is not a book of advice, but a true suite of instructions to bring about the possibilities inside each of us. It is a set of tools that, if utilized, brings about true personal freedom. There are also exercises to help you get to that place inside you that is screaming to come alive. Life is a gift. Why not get past the wrappings and into the heart of it? Let's learn the art of living out loud!

Chapter 1

Accept Yourself
(Who Are You Really?)

*If you really want things to change,
accept yourself. Doing this means being willing
to look at yourself deeply and to act
courageously on what you find.*

How did we get so far off track anyway? We want to be accepted by others, to fit in, to be noticed or recognized. Because of this many of us we have allowed ourselves to be conditioned by others to accept less in our lives, to accept untruths, and to generally disregard our dreams, desires, opinions, and even the experiences we want in our lives. No more!

Generationally speaking, we come from backgrounds that were filled with the expectations of our parents, caregivers, and the like. In most cases our parents and caregivers did their very best to give us what they thought we needed. They gave us the life tools they had, but honestly much of the time their life toolbox was missing some very basic skills. They were raised in a generation when authority was never questioned, period. The rules were followed, period—even when those rules were not in everyone's best interest, but in the interest of others. Our predecessors lived in a simple time when it occurred to very few that there was more to life than there was.

In most of our families we were told that we should do more, try harder, find our singular purpose in life and be the best at it. Unfortunately we weren't ever told what it looked like when we got there. We were given a road map with lots of traffic rules and no destinations.

Further, we were expected to behave in certain ways, to follow the social norms of the times, and God forbid we should express our real feelings. If we did, we were reprimanded or punished just for telling the truth. We were told we weren't being good girls or boys. We weren't encouraged to talk about things that hurt us. On the contrary, we were told to be quiet or ignored altogether. So we learned to bury that pain.

If people we encountered were different somehow or didn't fit the social norm, we were taught to shun them. We were basically taught that if they weren't like us, they were weird or simply not acceptable. Judgment became prevalent in our lives.

Many of our religions taught us that we had to be subservient, that we were blemished by the sins of man against a powerful God who would strike us down if we did not obey. That we were weak beings who must strive to atone for our sins—basically, that we were sinners from the word go.

I remember when I was a small child attending private school, and I had to go to confession weekly to report my sins to the parish priest. Confession was mandatory. I remember asking one of the nuns once if I didn't have any sins would I have to go to confession. She said everyone sinned and I absolutely must go. The problem was that I was just a little kid, and I had become so conforming out of fear of a vengeful God that I had to make up sins to confess.

Kneeling on the stone dais doing penance for sins I hadn't committed seemed like a paradox even then. I would justify the punishment by the fact that I had lied to the priest about my sins. So there I was, praying like crazy to atone for sins I would not have committed had I not been forced to do so! Instead of teaching me to be honest, they taught me to lie, even when the situation was a supposedly sacred, time-honored ritual.

As we conformed to these "acceptable" behaviors, slowly and steadily our sense of self became confused and even buried. We learned not to show our feelings because it was easier—and safer—than the conflict we might face if we did. We learned early on to defend ourselves by telling white lies—or even bigger ones—to those around us.

Similarly, we learned to lie to ourselves about this whole process. After all, we wanted to believe that we were good people, achieving all that was expected of us! Over time, being dishonest with others and ourselves became a habit, and somewhere in all of those little lies we lost touch with who we really are.

We were undermined in every direction of our development. Damned if we did, and damned if we didn't. Naturally, we began to look to our peers to tell us how we fit in, how we were doing, and whether we were right or wrong. We began to look externally for approval and validation of most everything we did or said. Some of us would have done nearly anything to feel we belonged or were accepted.

But here is the kicker—those we asked could answer us from only their own frames of reference. Their tool sets weren't exactly or necessarily full either, so it was the blind leading the blind.

Because of this, many of us find ourselves floundering, lost, misdirected—not knowing who we are or what we want and still trying to be a good girl or boy, whatever the heck that means! We strive to please people who really don't know any more than we do, and as a result we become unrecognizable to ourselves. We become unsatisfied, lack the fullness of our joy, and ultimately begin searching for an elusive . . . something . . . yet we aren't sure what that is. Needless to say our groping in the dark for the unknown isn't always a pretty picture.

Still, we look to others to fill our perceived emptiness, to validate us or offer their approval. In doing this, we give our power away thinking that we never had any anyway. We have come to see ourselves as alone in the world, separate from everyone and everything. We imagine that the experiences we have couldn't possibly be understood by anyone else. And of course in our separateness grows our deep and often painful sense of aloneness. From our feelings of isolation can come self-defensive behaviors that cause us the very problems we want to avoid, and our situations are compounded with disappointment after disappointment.

The Truth May Hurt, But at Least It's Mine!

As we closed ourselves off, defining our experiences by how deep our pain was, or how disappointed we were, we wished and hoped for more excellent experiences to come our way. In the meantime, we became unsure of what we wanted. We weren't even sure we deserved it because we couldn't see our value, so we developed this deep sense of being unfulfilled. We began to feel like we should be doing something else with our lives or that something greater is just around the corner, but beyond that we didn't have a clue how to get from here to there.

The only way out of this mess is to tell the truth—first to ourselves and then to others.

This brings me back to my original question. Who are you really? Do you remember? Did you ever know? What do you want in life?

> The greatest, most powerful words
> anyone can say in life are "I accept."

To embrace yourself just as you are without needing to be anything but the true you—and without the need to please anyone else.

If you really want things to change, accept yourself. Whoever you are, whatever that looks like, just accept you as you. No strings, no pretenses, no expectations, no preconceptions, no judgment. Just be willing to experience yourself undiluted by everyone else's opinions. Of course, you can't just think it and make it so; you have to do your part to make your life what you want, and this part is a process, not a single act. Self-acceptance is a way of life. It is about staying true to *you* no matter what.

> The truth is that in every given moment
> we have lived, we have done the best we could.
> There are no mistakes, only opportunities
> to learn, change, or grow.

The first step to realizing who we are is to stop the untruths, to ourselves as well as others. Untruths begin when we are uncomfortable inside ourselves based on our experiences and interactions with others. Mentally, as we try to justify our experiences, we toss our experiences around in our brains like a washing machine on a spin cycle. The information never resolves because it is caught in a cycle of repetitive thinking that lacks logic and, therefore, sense. Ultimately our brains will make leaps and assumptions in order to create a coherent and understandable version of our experiences . . . and that "logic" is often far from the truth.

*We don't realize that no amount of rationalization
or cyclic thinking leads to truth.
Resolution is only an illusion for satisfaction of the ego.*

In an effort to be comfortable, to fit in, to feel important, we tell ourselves any number of untruths. We might tell ourselves that, even though someone isn't treating us right, they don't really mean it. (Oh yes, they do!) We might tell ourselves we are loved and wanted by someone who doesn't give us the first indication this is so. (Because the truth is they don't love us— we just want them to so badly!) We might tell ourselves that our significant other would never fool around on us when in fact there is blatant evidence to the contrary. (We don't want to accept we could be betrayed like that!) We might tell ourselves we're hard workers when in fact we're slacking off because no one is watching. (We really hate our jobs but haven't found the gumption to look for something else.) We might tell ourselves we're great parents when we barely spend any time with our children. (We need to be convinced we are good in every way so we lie to ourselves.) We might tell ourselves almost anything if it makes us more comfortable with our experiences, as if things seemed to fit better in our lives.

With each self-deception we fall further and further away from knowing who we are. If we are to know what we want, even what we need, we must be able to first *recognize* those wants and needs.

It is time to stop pretending that everything is just fine. Time to let go of the illusion that we are something we are not and find out just who is hiding behind all the distractions our lies have created.

If what we feel inside is equal to what we feel on the outside, then we are in good shape, balanced and honest with ourselves. When we are not being honest with ourselves our body begins to give us signals. When we experience an untruth, our bodies tell us. One of the first things that happens is we hold our breaths. We get tension in the chest or shoulders and neck, or we get that lurching feeling inside as if a herd of elephants just stampeded across our equilibrium. Mood shifts can be another sign that we are not really comfortable with what is going on—but aren't dealing with it.

So when our bodies signal that we are out of truth, we need to start paying attention. Stop. Right then. Take a literal step back, and ask yourself: To what is my body reacting? Catch it in the now. What was your last thought? What was it about? Was that really the truth, or did you just tell yourself that so you would feel better? Listen. What do you hear? No, I don't mean the birds outside the window or the traffic going by. What do you hear inside of you? What is your body saying to you? Find the untruth and tell yourself the real truth—even if it means that things are not going to be the same anymore. Especially then.

It's Time to Live Out Loud!

Learning to tell the truth can be tough because we can feel exposed, unsafe. The best way to go about recognizing your truth is one truth at a time. First of all, listen to your body. It is your first line of defense. When there is an untruth at hand, your body will tense, usually in the chest or the solar plexus. You might find that you are holding your breath, your stomach is tight, or . . . well, you know your body more than you think you do.

Find the deceptions inside you. Change those untruths to real truths by getting honest with yourself. If someone is treating you badly but you've made excuses for them time and again, why not admit to yourself that person doesn't show you respect? Even further, perhaps their treatment is abusive. Is that what you want? If you have been the target of unkind behavior in someone close to you but haven't addressed it with them—because you don't really want to know the answer or you've convinced yourself that you can't possibly be right, address this with yourself. For example: Did you promise to go somewhere when you really didn't want to go only because you wanted to be accepted; or maybe you thought someone wouldn't like you if you didn't go? Listen to your reluctance to go, and *don't go!*

If you don't have respect for yourself and your needs, why would anyone else?

So you begin to get the picture. Honesty applies in every nook and cranny of our lives.

As you get the hang of recognizing the real truth, put your newfound way of being into action with others as well. For instance, when you go out to lunch with friends and they suggest a restaurant you don't like, or you're in the mood for something else, speak up politely but confidently. Suggest the place where you want to go. Remember, you only get what you ask for! NO one will hate you because you have a preference!

If you really want to eat there, but no one else does, be prepared to go to your selected eatery by yourself. Do it with love for yourself, not in a snit. Similarly, if your family wants to go to the movies, and the only film they want to see doesn't appeal to you but another you've wanted to see for months does, go to the one you want. Why sit through a movie you don't want to see? It's not like you'd have a lot of quality conversation during the film anyway. Go to the one you want and meet everyone afterward. It isn't a crime if you do. The real crime is when you give in time and time again at your own expense while trying to please everyone else. Honestly, would they do that for you?

Again, do it with a smile and assure them it really is okay; you'll see each other later.

With each small truth you tell, the greatness of your power as a human being returns. And real power is gentle power. It is not aggressive or threatening. It is all about living your truth. The key to telling the truth is simple; the message is entirely dependent upon its delivery. In other words, how we say things makes all the difference in how they are heard. If we feel threatened and we send our words out as a jab, we are going to get jabbed back. If we deliver our message sincerely and without drama or trauma, that message will have a chance of being heard as clearly as it was intended.

With each truth we tell, we take back our sense of self.

Exercise:
Where Is My Attention?

Find a place that is quiet and comfortable. Close your eyes and be still. Direct your attention inward. What do you hear? Is it the chatter of a million thoughts running through your mind, or something deeper? The chatter is part of your defense system that keeps the truth from reaching you. Try telling it to be silent. If the chatter continues, ask yourself: Where is my attention? Put your attention on you and nothing else. Listen to your breath. Inhale slowly, exhale slowly and deliberately. As you breathe inward, command to hear only the truth. As you exhale, expel the lies that have hidden within you. No more excuses, no more misinformation that leads you nowhere. Now, what do you hear?

You can do this any time you want, even every day. It takes only a few minutes. Remember to breathe as you command truth in your life, your very being. As you exhale, expel the untruths that you hold—about anyone or anything that is keeping you from being who you want to be. Who you are.

Chapter 2

Understand Your Purpose
(It's Not What You Think!)

*Our life purpose is not a singular event,
but a collective of what we have experienced
in every moment we have lived.*

So, you don't know where you are going in life? You want so much but in spite of your fantasies nothing quite shakes out the way that you want it. You have searched and searched and don't understand what your purpose might be. You have asked a lot of people but what they tell you just doesn't fit no matter how hard you try. That is because what they are giving you isn't yours.

To understand our purpose we must first realize one of the most significant statements this book can offer: *Nothing ever happens outside of now. What was, has been. What hasn't yet been is merely imagined or speculated.*

Let me repeat that: Nothing ever happens outside of now.

This one little sentence can change your life entirely. Most of us spend all our time worrying about what we did or didn't do or what might happen or not happen. Our attention is not in the now, but in the past or future. But creation is always talking to us; it communicates with us in real time with cutting-edge information that is congruous and never ceasing. When our attention is elsewhere, we are not present in the now, and so we miss opportunities and signs that could have easily taken us to what we wanted.

When we are not completely present in this now, the synchronicities, those magic little miracles in every moment, also go unnoticed. We aren't grounded and are probably not even completely in our bodies. How could we possibly know what our life purpose is when we don't even occupy a singular moment?

Life is nothing more than a series of moments tied together by events that create a sense of experience.

All complexity is nothing more than an entanglement of simple situations.

The bottom line is that nothing is complex and everything is simple.

Each moment is a simple situation. It only becomes complex or challenging when we make it so. Our minds have learned to defend us because that was how we were conditioned. Our minds actually work to defend us before our thoughts even arrive and are recognized as such. Not only that but our minds are a bit insane. They create pieces of logic that are untrue in order to make sense out of what they don't understand. In other words, our logical minds are chronic liars!

Communication is going on constantly within and around us. In and out, we receive and transmit information to all creation, telling it what our experiences are and what we want. As we do, we expend and receive energy.

Because of these energy exchanges we are literally never the same from one moment to the next. The symphony of our layered makeup may have a few new notes, or a slightly changed rhythm. The same thing happens when we interact with others. We exchange energy with them as we talk, as we express our emotions; even our movements communicate through the expression of energy. Others, even total strangers, receive our energy just as we receive theirs. And as this occurs we may never know just how much we have affected another person.

Our life purpose is not a singular event, but a collective of all that we experience in our journeys. Each of us in essence holds a particular place in Universal reality. Because of this, each of us is a part of the balance of all that is. There is no other who can maintain your particular place within creation but you.

Each time you interact with another and each time they with you, there is an exchange of energies that changes both of you forever. What you have given, and what you have received, changes both of your energetic structures. Know this: In a sweet and simple yet much grander way you may have changed that person's life completely.

One of my favorite stories is that of a woman who was at the post office to pay her bills. As she stood in line waiting for her turn, she contemplated her death. She was going to go home to commit suicide. Her husband, the love of her life, had died unexpectedly and she was devastated. She had been abandoned as a child, then adopted and abused mentally, emotionally, and sexually by her adoptive parents. Her husband had been her salvation. He had been the first person in her life who had truly loved her unconditionally, and she had learned the meaning of love through him. Now she had lost him. He was gone, so today was going to be it. She was definitely leaving the planet.

Right about then a woman in the line next to her turned, met her eyes, and smiled at her—a quick cursory smile, like most all of us do to be polite. The woman then turned and went about her business, got her stamps, and left. To this day that wonderful kind woman has no idea that her small gesture of kindness saved a very fragile life.

The distraught woman had felt noticed. Someone cared enough to smile at her. In the midst of her grief she had found an island of kindness and she decided that maybe life was worth living after all. She decided to live.

Because of a total stranger she changed the entire direction of her life. She ultimately moved to a foreign country, where she teaches crafts so the locals can supplement their meager incomes. She also teaches children at the nearby school skills like how to make jewelry, and how to grow herbs; she assists the villagers in their farming techniques. The numbers of lives that have been enriched by that one smile are countless.

One singular now . . . Wow.

We never really know how we affect others. When we remember to act with intention, to mean what we say and say what we mean, we become that which we intend. We also become the moment. As we do, every expression, every thought, every move that we make, every feeling that we have, and every word that we say becomes reality.

Our purpose in life is not singular by any means. It is every separate moment that we exist.

Exercise:
Learning to Be Now

Sit somewhere comfortable. Imagine that before you is a pyramid. The pyramid is a hologram created of light. If a pyramid is hard for you to imagine, try picturing first a triangle of light. Imagine you can see through it. Project your attention to the inside of the pyramid. Breathe easily, in, out, in, out. You might find that your breath begins to cool. If it does, you have found the center of the pyramid.

Do you hear anything? A tone, perhaps? That tone is how you sound in all of creation. It is your harmonic signature. Being inside the pyramid allows you to safely experience yourself away from your body as a clear consciousness without the chatter of your mind. This space, this state, is you in clarity, unpolluted by earthly defenses. It is the essence of you in a safe place, where there are no threats to defend against. Stay there as long as you wish. Relax. Let yourself experience you without boundaries. You are safe. When you have relaxed fully and allowed yourself to become the pyramid, you will have truly become the infinite now.

Chapter 3

Recognize Your Patterns
(Oh No, Not Again!)

Patterns are quite recognizable when we step back and really look at our relationships and our habits objectively. Once we have recognized these tendencies and have awareness of our fears, we can let them go. Then, no one can hurt us in that way ever again.

How do we change our experience? How do we find our fears and, further, how do we get rid of them?

First of all we must learn to recognize our patterns. Patterns are situations that come up over and over again—different face, different day—where the underlying dynamics at work stem from the same source. These patterns often denote underlying fears that we have not dealt with. They cycle through our lives giving us opportunities to make a different choice, to change our response to a given situation, or even to conquer our fears, and most often we don't recognize them.

There is a good chance that patterns come from within our family's examples of behaviors. It is quite common to replicate the behaviors we learned as children from our parents or care-givers. Often we learn by example, and those examples aren't always particularly healthy for us.

For instance, our relationships with others often present very recognizable patterns. How many friendships have come and gone that left you saying something like, "Why do I always attract these kinds of people? The same situations happen over and over and I just don't get it!" That is because you are choos-ing people over and over again who give you the opportunity to choose differently! As soon as you do, the patterns stop. It is really that simple.

Another kind of pattern we often encounter is repeti-tive issues. Issues of honesty or integrity or betrayal are the most common. How many times have you been in a situation where you felt someone took advantage of you? Maybe he borrowed money he never paid back. Or maybe she wasn't true to her word. Maybe you felt betrayed by what he did or didn't do.

Just when you think things are going well, on another day with another person it happens again. And again. What aren't you getting? In this case, fear that has created a lack of self-worth has conquered once again. But since it keeps happening, you must deserve it, right? No!

When we don't value ourselves, we are sitting ducks for oth-ers to mirror back to us that very sense of worthlessness! They treat us as if we don't matter, as if we were "less than" or don't know as much. We get taken advantage of. This mirroring we receive from others will be exactly what we feared in the first place. Worse, we become victims of our own creations!

*If you don't value yourself,
why should anyone else? The patterns
perpetuated by your fears will spiral
over and over again until you have conquered
your fears . . . or succumbed to them.*

Patterns are quite recognizable when we step back and really look at our relationships and our habits objectively. Once we have recognized these tendencies and have awareness of our fears, then no one can ~~hurt you~~ us in that way anymore. Unfortunately, it is what we won't look at or can't see that perpetuates the cycle time and again. To follow are just a few types of patterns you may recognize in yourself or someone around you.

You Deserve So Much More

Definition: Victim: one who allows others to use or abuse them with or without permission at their expense and without reward.

What we are talking about here is victimization. Being a victim has no rewards and a whole lot of pain. The truth is that when we are victims we aren't taking responsibility for our own lives even though we think at the time that we are doing our very best. We are often looking to others to make those choices for us, but instead they take advantage of us and often even abuse us in any number of ways.

Being a victim means that your fear is paralyzing you!

Your fear leaves you with a sense of powerlessness because you believe that others have more of something than you do. That is far from the truth. Still, you don't speak up when you disagree or want something different because it is too hard. You fear the consequences.

Further, staying in the victim role only serves to attract other bullies who will treat you exactly as you have invited. When we are in victim mode, it is like we are sending out signals to others that they can take what they want, do what they want to us. And they will. To believe that you are anything less than perfect is detrimental to your experience as a human being. You are perfection, hands down, no question.

Victimization is a pattern that can be broken only when the victim has had enough abuse and is ready to become something other than a target for others who want to feel more powerful.

If you are in a victim role, whether it is in a relationship or life in general, break the pattern. Stop doing what everyone else wants. Start telling your truth even though doing so may be one of the scariest things you have ever done. Make different choices. Yes, others did mean to hurt you because you made it easy. Stop deferring to others. Stand up for yourself. Begin to reward yourself for even the smallest of successes. Recognize that part of you really does want change, and act on it. Give yourself some credit.

The best way to change your life is to change your mind.

Seriously. Our fears help us to develop belief systems that are disempowering. When we begin to believe something different, not only does our entire perspective change, our lives change!

Sometimes when we are in a victim role everything seems impossible. It is difficult to stand up and make the change. This is, of course, not the truth; it is only a perception. Anything is possible if we believe it.

Sometimes, though, powerlessness sneaks up on us. We become embroiled in it slowly, losing our self-respect, until one day we look up and can't see our way out. Someone, or more than someone, may have manipulated us to the point we no longer know what is true. We are in way over our heads with mixed feelings and emotions. We want to think the best of people but they aren't acting rationally.

If you feel your situation is out of control to a dangerous point, especially in an abusive relationship, and you feel unsafe and your situation is hurting you, please get help. If someone is hurting you it is *not* okay, no matter how many times they say they didn't mean it or they apologize. Get help. Not your best friend's help. Help by people who will keep you safe in the transition. There are many different agencies who offer social services like counseling, safe houses, any number of possibilities to help you gain control of your life.

You deserve only the best of everything.

You are a child of creation, made of the same stuff that all others are made of. Therefore there cannot be anyone who is lesser or greater than you!

You have the inalienable right to experience life on your own terms. It is your birthright. You didn't come to this world to be insignificant. You came to experience life at its fullest!

The Do-Gooder

Another pattern of behavior that masks the truth is defined beautifully as I call the Do-Gooder. The Do-Gooder spends most of their time flitting around, doing for others in a selfless sacrifice of time and personal resources. Do-Gooders can't sit still. Doing for others is a way of avoiding feeling one's own pain. Do-Gooders work mostly on the surface, hiding their inner feelings by focusing instead on someone else's problems. The Do-Gooder waits on others hand and foot, helping them clean up their personal messes and generally working hard to be the good girl or boy.

Being a Do-Gooder brings a false sense of value or accomplishment. Do-Gooders go home at night feeling satisfied and valuable for all they have contributed on the behalf of others. In the meantime, they haven't done much of anything about their own stuff, and more often than not they are sadly unappreciated by those they have helped. By doing for everyone else, living the reality that others are creating, the Do-Gooder feels a false sense of value and reward.

On the road of life, we subconsciously create situations so we can learn from them. Sometimes those situations are very hard. And yet, when we get ourselves into these messes we know exactly who to call . . . the Do-Gooder!

And, bless their hearts, Do-Gooders don't remember how to say no, and so will drop everything in their own lives to rescue the troubled friend or family member . . . or even a total stranger— when most often they really need to be rescued themselves!

But what the Do-Gooder doesn't realize is that, by carrying the weight of someone else's situation, they are robbing that person of the fullness of the experience he or she created in order to learn and change. And then, later on, the person who was in trouble and got bailed out by the Do-Gooder will inevitably call again with similar issues because they didn't learn the first time how to solve their own problems because someone rescued them!

You see this pattern a lot in families. Well-meaning parents rescue their children over and over, and then don't understand why that son or daughter continues to get into trouble. For instance, a grown son can't seem to hold a job, and regularly goes to Mom and Dad for an infusion of money. Mom and Dad feel sorry for their son, who "tries so hard," so they give him the cash—with a lecture about getting a job—and then the cycle repeats over and over again. The son doesn't learn, and neither do the parents; what is "the right thing to do" for them in fact enables their son *not* to work—and not to live his own life.

If you think you might be a Do-Gooder, the first thing you can do is stop *doing* and start watching. Becoming a conscious observer removes you from the drama and the trauma, and allows you to see things for what they are. Instead of running to the rescue all the time, the greatest way you can assist someone is not by *doing* for them, but by giving them the tools to help themselves.

For instance, give suggestions toward resolution: "Here is where you can get what you need, here are some ideas about how to make this situation different." Or, "Here are some observations for you that I noticed the last three times I helped you with similar problems." And then let them choose to resolve their situation or not. Let them be responsible. Either they will be, or they will go looking for someone else to fix things for them. Either way, you are no longer caught in a spiral of exhausting, unfulfilling doing.

> Doing for others in the above ways
> doesn't give you value, it enslaves you.

The Do-Gooder is really only trying to placate that good little girl or boy inner child who never really felt enough recognition. The key here is to give yourself fair recognition—real acknowledgment—without the need to receive the kudos from someone else. Give yourself the value that you give others. Let others help you. (What a concept!) Pretty soon saying no won't be so hard!

Most of all, be still, feel your feelings, be honest with yourself, and deal with whatever comes up—so that you can stop running from yourself, and start living authentically.

The Charming User

Opposite to the Do-Gooder is the User. Users are those who have, for whatever reason, become dependent personalities. They are needy and don't believe they have what it takes to take care of themselves on all levels.

Users generally are very personable, charming in fact, and love to talk. They sit back and consciously or subconsciously watch for opportunities to get what they need from others rather than on their own merits. Often this behavior is masked by an expressive and charismatic nature. They will become your best friend—and it will cost you.

Becoming a User results from fear of real commitment and/or extending personal effort. This comes from an unrecognized sense of self-loathing. At the same time, the User has a false sense of self-worth, instilled by self-deception somewhere along the line.

Users are not at all honest with themselves, and will be completely convinced that getting something from someone without giving back is the absolutely most right thing they have ever done. They will have a thousand excuses why getting something for nothing is right—if the situation is even discussed. On the other hand, the User doesn't feel this way deep down inside. Inside, the User is afraid to commit to whatever it takes to be a success. The User feeds off of the success of others, feeling important by association. Taking becomes a pattern.

When Users have "used up" a person or group, they will find a new set of people to draw from. If ever asked what happened, the User will mumble some lame excuse and change the subject with the usual charm. This is all part of the pattern. Users often move around a lot so as not to get caught in this game. Of course this is part of the illusion, because everyone else usually sees Users for who they really are.

It's not that Users are lazy; they just truly don't have the sense of self-worth or self-confidence to dive in like everyone else. Users are envious because they haven't yet realized that the power to create is within them. To give to Users is to enable and perpetuate their habits of taking—and, worse, perpetuate their fears.

If this sounds like you, and you are willing to recognize these traits in yourself, the best thing you can do is to begin to empower yourself. You can begin by first admitting this is your pattern; second, you can learn to give. Start by accomplishing even small commitments to which you have no agenda of receiving. You hold onto things way too tightly because you see your value in them. But these things have no value if you don't. Start giving so you can receive a different type of reward in life . . . true satisfaction and a whole lot of self-value!

Cat on a Hot Tin Roof

Another pattern that is difficult to break is what I call Cat on a Hot Tin Roof. This pattern, which is based upon fear of being hurt (again!), is a pattern of avoidance. It stems from the fear of either facing one's deeper feelings or having one's emotions exposed. Those with this pattern often perceive that showing their feelings is unsafe and will leave them vulnerable.

In constant motion, the Cat on a Hot Tin Roof is usually highly intelligent, using those smarts as a diversion from emotions. They are often workaholics, or flit from one activity to another, living on the surface and never allowing anyone to know their real feelings or perceptions.

A great example of this kind of behavior occurred when I was teaching an exercise in one of my workshops. In the exercise, students had to find objects that represented their regrets, fears, perceptions of mistakes, and past injuries of every kind. Once the objects were collected, we formed a circle and, one at a time, each person had the opportunity to go into the center of the circle to consciously let go of—and give up—all of that past pain.

One of my students entered the circle but, instead of standing there, really present with the ceremony, she kept walking round and round inside the circle. She was being playful, not appearing to take the exercise seriously—smiling, being her usual jovial self. She was also extremely distracting, both to herself and to the group.

"Be still," I gently commanded.

She stopped, looked up, eyes wide . . . and immediately fell apart. The tears that she had avoided for a lifetime came pouring out, and afterward, she was calm inside for the first time ever. She hadn't even known she had a pattern of avoidance.

The best way to break a pattern of avoidance is first to realize that it exists. Since the skill of steering clear of one's powerful emotions also results in a lot of self-denial, this pattern really requires a mammoth effort at self-honesty. Once it is found, though, life can take on great depths of feeling and meaning.

The Isolator

Isolators doesn't want to be seen. They are like little mice, bright and aware, hiding where no one can see them, coming out only when no one is really looking.

Avoiding attention, Isolators are always hiding, in a book, or some project, holding in feelings to the point of revealing little outward expression. The amazing thing is that when Isolators finally do speak, the depth of their awareness, observations, or knowledge is often a great surprise to others. Their perceptions about others are often brilliant, but are most often kept to themselves. There is much lurking deep in there!

Isolators are nearly invisible. This is due to the fear of being exposed, of having feelings show or thoughts expressed that can then be judged by someone else or used against them. Isolators believe it is only safe to be quiet and unavailable. Invisible. Of course invisibility may accomplish the obvious, but this kind of behavior really limits life experience. After all, what doesn't get in also doesn't get out. The greatest depth of life experience is avoided—and missed out on. Life becomes a series of fantasies or dreams that, even if participated in, are never quite fulfilling.

The Isolator fills his or her time with distractions such as a good book or analytic behavior. Everything needs to be understood so there are no surprises. But there always are.

If you are one of these delicate people, start putting yourself into small situations that stretch your comfort zone. Let yourself be seen a bit, even if you are not comfortable. What you will find is that you are beautiful, and when you are seen, others will see your beauty. People will like you because they will be able to know you—and your hideout won't beckon so loudly.

The Bully (aka the Know-It-All)

Another behavioral pattern that arises from fear is, believe it or not . . . the Bully (also known as the Know-it-all). This behavior comes from deep fear of not being good enough. This person usually comes from a family background in which they were seriously disempowered by a parent or parents who were of similar dominant personality. The general tendency is to cover all sense of vulnerability by becoming omnipotent. Bigger than life, louder than loud. This behavior often manifests as rude, vociferous—acting as if their way is the only way no matter what the cost to others. They have to be right no matter what, always needing to have the last word. Worse, they are great BS artists, seeming gregarious when they are really tearing you down in more subtle ways. They come across as Know-it-alls.

Being this way of course, is to cover up the fact that they are absolutely terrified of being wrong. Believe it or not, this type of personality pattern is one of the most emotionally sensitive. Criticism injures and infuriates them because their insecurities are so deep they often go completely unrecognized. Everything becomes everyone else's fault and responsibility. Even though the Bully doesn't really know everything, they have convinced themselves they do and will talk right over anyone who tries to express an alternative opinion.

The Bully will bark at others from the perspective of absolute righteousness about how things are or should be done. They have such a sense of self-righteousness that they often cause hard feelings in families and social circles. They directly inflict pain on others most often verbally or by withholding attention, and doing this makes them feel very powerful. Of course, the fact is that is far from the truth.

The general tendency people have when facing this kind of personality is to avoid interaction with the Bully whenever possible in order to avoid a confrontation or argument. The typical response to the Bully is to go along with them and then run fast to get away. The problem is that when we do this we actually enable their behavior.

On the other hand, Bullies or Know-it-alls are also at times very generous people. They will surprise you with presents or money and do so with great fanfare. They are gregarious people who are hard to avoid. On the inside there is a lot of pent-up emotion, feelings that have not been expressed because, again, it feels unsafe to do so. The Bully or Know-it-all is generally a marshmallow inside when you get past the façade.

If you recognize yourself in this pattern, my suggestion is that you learn to relax. You no longer have anything to prove. Your pain is not serving you and is generally sabotaging your relationships with others. No one is watching over your shoulder anymore. The only person you must please is yourself. Be gentle to you.

You are a powerful and magnificent being of creation and that is good enough. Learning to be truthful with yourself is the number one priority. The second is to learn to have compassion for yourself. It is okay that you hurt inside; it is not okay to hurt others because you do. If you can find compassion for yourself, you will have it for others, and will begin to understand that damage is done when you bark at others or overrun them with your perceived power. Learn to laugh at yourself, with yourself. It is never too late.

Of course the above examples are just a few types of patterns of behavior. The kinds of patterns we develop are endless, but for the most part are familiar to all of us. If we can develop an awareness of those patterns we can also begin to recognize our fears. Fear isn't reality. This is. This now.

Exercise:
Defining and Changing Patterns

What kinds of situations have repeated for you over the years? Do you attract the same personality types and then find the relationships unbearable? Are you experiencing similar behaviors from your friends, loves, others? Have you ever said something like, "I guess I have to keep doing this until I get it right"? The answer is likely yes!

Once you identify your repetitive situations, ask yourself how you can react or respond differently next time—because there will be a next time. Once you change how you react or respond, the pattern will stop.

Chapter 4

Stop Being Afraid
(You Are Sabotaging Your Life!)

*Fear mostly remains in the background
limiting our experiences by keeping us
in narrow perspectives. Once we recognize
and deal with our fears we are free to be or do
whomever and whatever we desire.*

Fear underlies everything we do. It runs our show from behind, driving us to choices we regret, opportunities we miss, often to the point of grief for what was or what could have been.

Some of the common fears we experience are:

- I won't be loved. (Who would love me?)
- I might be abandoned. (No one loves me. No one wants me . . .)
- What if I am rejected? (Well, I knew I wouldn't fit in.)
- Will I be judged? (I am doing the best that I can . . . aren't I?)

- If I am not loved then I will be alone. (I am terrified of being alone!)

- Will I succeed? Am I good enough? Probably not. (Doesn't success mean being responsible?)

- Do I deserve what I want? (I am not worth what I want . . . I am not enough even by my own standards.)

- I am afraid to bear responsibility. (I don't know enough, am not enough . . . what if I make a mistake? What if it is all just too much?)

- What if someone notices me? (God! If I am seen I am no longer invisible! Who do I have to be then? What if I screw up? I like being invisible. It's safer!)

Of course these are just a few samples; the "complete" list is endless. But the truth is that fear is not a reality, it is a what-if. Fear causes the paralysis of our natural progression—and is the cause of all failure.

Most of our fear is subconscious. Even though we don't realize it, fear drives the vast majority of our actions, behaviors, choices, even our life paths. We make our decisions with our fears biting us in the rear end, reminding us of our disappointments and failures. Because of that, we often make choices from a place of weakness. We make our choices reflexively and without much thought based upon our history, patterns of behavior and the underlying fears that result from those past experiences. These choices often lead us down a road that absolutely validates why we were afraid.

In other words, fear begets fear. It becomes a cyclic set of behaviors that become literal addictions. We make the same fearful choices over and over again, completely missing the fact that we are in a pattern of discomfort. And then we wonder why things aren't the way we meant or wanted them to be. As we decide our life directions, do we take the easy road, the one that is most familiar, or do we take the high road, the one with more difficult opportunities to learn differently but also greater prospects for the life we really want?

A lot of us choose comfortable discomfort. We choose within our comfort zone, which really isn't comfortable at all, but it is all we know and what we think of as safe, right? Wrong!

If we are afraid, then we perceive that for some reason we aren't safe. But since our uncomfortable situations are at least predictable, we repeatedly choose them to create a false sense of safety—even though we are unhappy.

Our false sense of safety gives us the illusion that we are in control. We know what to expect . . . and feel relieved to have life so predictable, so contained . . . Not!

Part of the illusion of control is that we set ourselves up for disappointment. We do this by having expectations. When things don't turn out like we expected, our fears are validated. Further, no one else knows what we expect because it is our private little secret. They don't have a clue how to participate with us so in the process of trying to control everything we instead create total failure.

Setting ourselves up for failure of any kind, whether it is disappointment or reinforcement of our beliefs of not being good enough or deserving of what we hoped for is, in simple terms, self-sabotage. This self-sabotage proves over and over again that all of our fears are true after all! When things don't work out everything that we feared is confirmed. But it doesn't have to be that way!

Exercise:
Identifying Your Fears

A word of warning: this exercise takes honesty. It's not about getting the answers right; it isn't a test. At the same time, it does require a hard, honest look at painful experiences you've had. This isn't about reliving the pain, or even wallowing in it. This is about allowing your own experiences to help you understand some of the root causes underlying the choices you've made. What brings you to repeat hurtful patterns? What have you been fighting all these years? What are your core fears? As painful as such contemplation may seem, try to approach this from a curious perspective. This exercise is intended to help you recognize the parts you play when fear presides over your life, and to show you how to truly free yourself from fear.

To do this exercise, carve out some time in a private space where you won't be interrupted, and have a pen and blank paper handy. You're going to want to allow yourself to think of experiences that make your guts jump. You know the feeling . . . that lurch in your chest or your belly. The very experiences you don't like to think about—because they hurt— are the experiences that can best help you.

Usually when we have experiences that are uncomfortable, it's easy to blame those experiences on someone else, or on something we felt we couldn't help at the time. But this exercise isn't about what anyone else might have said or done. This exercise is only about you—your feelings, your reactions, your needs.

So here we go. Let yourself think of experiences that bring up that lurching feeling. Write down the first one that comes to mind. Not who did what or said what, just the experience. Here is an example: "I was in a relationship that didn't work out. He/She left me with no explanation and went on to someone else. I found out later that the new relationship had started while he/she was still with me." Write maybe three sentences saying, simply, what happened.

Now look at what you've written. What were the emotions you felt at the time? What had you been afraid would happen that happened anyway? Write those down too. If you look more closely at what you've written, see if you can whittle down your feelings into one or two words that succinctly describe your fears.

For the relationship example above, you might identify your core fears as:

- fear of abandonment
- fear of betrayal

Now that you've analyzed that experience and noted your core fears, do you think you can try another? The more you mine, the more you learn. Another example might be: "Everyone ganged up on me over something I said, and I tried so hard to fix it. But I was shunned anyway, and ultimately pushed out of the group."

Core fears for this experience might be:

- fear of judgment
- fear of rejection
- fear of abandonment

The goal of this exercise is to name the fears that drive you to do things you wouldn't otherwise do. For instance, imagine you were the person pushed out of the group in the example above. What fear might have caused you to "allow" the people in the group to push you away when you still wanted their acceptance? Why didn't you, or couldn't you, express your feelings and intentions to try to save the relationships? You may have slinked or faded away without objecting, or dug your hole deeper by shouting your hurt, or anger, or both. There was nothing wrong with what you said to them; others in the group just used it as an opportunity to gain false power. But there you were, fighting tooth and nail for them to accept you. And here you are, years later, still hurting over it while they have gone on with their lives and probably don't even remember the event.

Go to the next event in your life that brings up that awful physical feeling. Repeat the process until you have addressed all of the situations that you can think of.

When you are finished, look over the fears you wrote down. You will find that the same words repeat over and over again. These are your core fears. Now that you have recognized them, and owned them, you can let them go. Have compassion for yourself for allowing these fears to run your life, and make a pact with yourself that you are done with these fears.

The next time the patterns start to come up, you are more likely to recognize them—and choose from your power rather than your fear. Oh, and have a sense of humor about it. Laugh at yourself when you find those fears creeping up! You now know better! You aren't hiding from yourself anymore! The best news is that once you are aware of your fears, no one else can hurt you there anymore. This is living from within your vulnerabilities. If you have owned your fears, no one can use them against you.

Learning to be unafraid frees us to experience our lives to the fullest potential. Further, when we are not afraid, we can communicate with others honestly and fully. A lack of fear allows for open communication without editing!

Chapter 5

Find Your Passion
(Feeling Deeply Can Be Amazing)

*Passion ignites when we love. When we are open,
defenses down, there are no limits to how deeply
and fully we can feel. We can only experience real
passion when we relax and let ourselves become
free of self-imposed restrictions.*

The first thing to realize here is that passion is not an achievement. Passion is love in action.

So, life is boring. You feel like you're in a rut and don't know how to change that. Sometimes we think of passion much in the way that we look for the voice of God . . . a booming unmistakable blast from the heavens that is all encompassing. We think of passion as total bliss that fills us to the point of falling to our knees. The truth is that, in the same way that God doesn't shout at us in his huge voice, passion is often more subtle. Passion is often a feeling that starts in our very core and slowly (or quickly, depending upon the circumstances) fills first our heart space and then overflows outward through our bodies.

Passion is everything that we love. It is the feeling that fills us with joy and releases our emotions with such magnitude that we have to express them or we will bust. Remember how, on Christmas morning as you ran to see what Santa had brought, you were filled with excitement? Or how when you got your first bike you felt so big? Passion is like that.

Passion can also be depth of Spirit. As we allow ourselves to be in a place of feeling all that is sacred, we are overwhelmed with Grace, a feeling that both humbles and empowers us and often brings us to a point that we can barely stand. (I think this is why we have to kneel in church. When this kind of passion is felt, there is nowhere else to go but to crumple under the beauty of it and become immersed in Spirit.)

Passion can be pure love for another person, for an activity, for something small or large, or even for the sheer beauty of our world. To experience the intricacies of nature as each aspect of our world is created in a way that it is both separate and dependent. Look at the human body for instance. We are a complete biosystem that has multiple parts, each with a purpose, all dependent upon the others but contributive to the whole.

We have the ability to choose what we do or experience, the ability to move about in our world and experience as much of it as we desire. We choose how we feel and what we want all the while our bodies continue to support us as long as we give them the care that they need.

Passion for another person can also be profound when it is pure and allowed to come to the surface.

What we feel when we look into the eyes of our children is a form of passion. We want everything for them and would do anything to protect them.

A warrior is passionate against his enemy.

Religions create passionate belief.

Essentially, passion has many faces and is only experienced when we release the bondage that we have created to restrict the world from seeing our true nature. It happens when we allow ourselves to feel and fully express our hearts.

A lot of us seem to feel that we are not living our passions, that we are in a mundane life that seems to be status quo each day, predictable and lacking in depth or excitement. We want to feel inspired. We want to feel as if we matter and we want to live fully, yet there we sit, day after day, accepting life as the cards have been dealt. *This is a travesty!*

Hiding our passion is a betrayal of self. When we cover our emotions we distance ourselves, first from our own self-awareness and second from the awareness in every now of what others are experiencing or contributing with us. If we are to experience our passion we must first give up all preconception that it is something to be obtained. Passion is within us 24/7. It is inherent in us.

To be passionate is to be free of emotional bondage.

Most of us believe that passion is our purpose—that we have to achieve it. Our passion is not our purpose, it is our innate right. It is who we are when we allow our sacred selves to surface. When we let go of the illusion that we are separate and different from everyone else. We aren't, we can't be, nor will we ever be.

There is a vast difference between direction and purpose. Many people have gotten to the point that they are no longer excited about most things and often feel complacent, even morose, about their current circumstances. They have become so enmeshed in the herd, being like everyone else, that they are lost to the point of not recognizing their greatest motivational aspect, their passion. Now what?

We have learned that our purpose can be found in every moment, each now. But what about our passion? Our passion leads our direction, guides us, motivates us, and brings us pleasure in everything that we do.

The first question I ask people when they are feeling lost in life is, "What is your passion?" About nine-and-a-half out of ten people don't know the answer.

The truth is that passion is everything that we love. Passion dictates our direction when we allow ourselves the freedom of feeling to great depths. Passion allows us to give ourselves over completely to our actions and emotions. It fuels us when we are tired, and releases chemicals in our bodies that make us feel terrific. Passion gives us a spring in our step and the ability to spring out of bed in the morning with anticipation of a terrific day.

So why is it missing? How do we find that big, elusive feeling that brings exuberance to our everyday experiences? To find our passion, we must first understand why it is so hard to come by.

How We Become Desensitized

We have become an information world. We get world happenings almost in real time all of the time. As we witness wars and disasters, crime and punishment, indifference, overpopulation, undernourishment, disease, weather anomalies, and more part of our psyche turns away and closes down our sensitivity.

At the same time that we are closing down to the horrors in our world, there are ads and commercials blaring at us that if we buy a certain product it will make us beautiful, worthwhile, comfortable, loved, smarter, all of that and more. And our psyche believes some of that because color and movement, flashes of small bits of information all register on subliminal levels and convince us that what the ads are saying are true. Those ads contribute to the alteration of our belief systems.

At the same time, we have multiple technological devices: our cell phones, iPads, GPSs, laptops with us at all times feeding us information in real time about things we would have never needed to know or care about—but with all of the input, we crave more.

Information is plastered on buildings, billboards, buses, taxis, and in fact pretty much every available surface. We have too much coming at us to maintain the kind of sensitivity that we had in previous times.

We are becoming deculturalized. Our traditions are going by the wayside as their sacredness somehow gets lost in the bigger picture.

The world population is out of control; people are starving and going without basic needs while others waste everything.

Schools are beyond overcrowded, and we have all become numbers instead of human beings with names and lives and families and the potential to be in touch with ourselves and what is happening around us on a much finer scale.

Try watching a program on TV these days. There are more commercials running across the bottom of the screen, distracting us, than there are original programs.

With travel as easy as it is these days people travel all over the world. There is very little "us" and "them" anymore but a collective us, all of whom are after basically the same thing.

Like terminal cancer, corporations have taken over the world, defining our lives by their terms. There are drug ads everywhere, implying that we need something more than what we have and that we need it to be chemically induced. They tell us that we should talk to our doctors to obtain these medications. They show healthy, happy people without a care in the world, and make it seem that if we take drugs it is the best thing in the world for our life experience too. Personally I feel these commercials should be illegal. They aren't really about our health; they are about a healthy bottom line in the company's financials.

The corporate world in general employs scads of people in a race that no one can win, completely forgetting that it is the human element that keeps its wheels going. People become too stressed, too sick and tired to have any quality of life unless changes are made.

With our sensitivity bashed and battered we become emotionally shielded. We forget to nurture ourselves and we can't help but to subconsciously become emotionally closed. How can we feel passion when we are numbed on a daily basis by the entire world coming at us?

Relighting Your Fire

First of all we have to stop being so emotionally guarded. We hide our emotional expressions because we feel vulnerable and even exposed if we show our true feelings. We practically explode at times trying to hide how we feel, and when our feelings finally do come out, they are usually directed at someone who becomes the undeserving target of our rage. As we defend ourselves subconsciously we use up our vitality, the energy we have every day to apply to whatever we do, and our internal resources become taxed, even limited.

So what do we do about this? Bring our vulnerable selves into the world lock, stock, and barrel. When we operate from within our vulnerabilities no one can hurt us there anymore. We can reign unchallenged within ourselves. When we know our fears, as we have learned to do in chapter 3, have owned those fears and embraced them, we are no longer vulnerable except by our own perceptions.

Coming to the world honestly and without the old baggage brings lightness to our experience that we had forgotten. Honesty allows us to begin to feel again many of the emotions we had buried, stuffed, and forgotten. Having let go of fear frees us to feel infinitely and, further, to act on our feelings from the perspective of an innocent child.

We also need to self-nurture. So often we starve for simple safe touch, a nonthreatening experience, and peace. So we must do what we love, what opens our hearts, what comforts us. A long massage, a walk in the woods, a great book, anything that brings us back to center and inner comfort.

We must recall what brought passion to us in our past, like during our childhood when we were innocent and not guarded from life and everything was interesting and exciting.

A fun way to begin is to think about what you loved as a child. What brought you joy? What made you smile? What games did you play, stories did you tell, jokes did you share? What were your fantasies when you were a kid? Did you role play? Act out your favorite superhero or TV star? Who was it and what was it that you admired about them? Most likely it was that they acted courageously and without pause. They lived their true nature. You only stopped playing your childhood fantasies because someone somewhere decided that grownups couldn't play. They were idiots! Tap into those childhood memories. Let yourself grin.

Most of the people who I have assisted with this subject have immediately identified passion as having to do with other people. This saddens me. From my point of view, passion is an internal experience that brings animation and fulfillment to the expression of outward experience—life!

Passion is a lap full of puppies, a classic movie that jerks the emotions all over the board, leaving us always with a face full of tears or deep belly laughs. Passion is our spiritual self, that self that is limitless in heart and depth. Passion is a great conversation in which your ideas are challenged, and in the process come the inevitable aha moments. Passion is love and anger, grief and compassion. Passion is the penultimate emotion, bested only by love. Passion occurs any time that you feel love.

Quite frankly, if you aren't feeling passion, you are probably too busy doing for everyone else and haven't realized that receiving is just as important as giving. When we give and give without replenishing our resources we get tired to the core. When we are emotionally unfulfilled and tired we cannot find the depth of feeling that we so desire. To change this we must begin by learning how to command what we need and then gracefully receive it.

Receiving is about value. If we don't give ourselves the perception of value we only get what we believe. In other words, if we envision ourselves as having lack then we receive lack. Lack finds us. After all, everything that we seek seeks us. What we intend is truth . . . at least our truth. We seek validation, a sense of belonging, a feeling of value, but if we don't know how to receive what we have asked for, how can we possibly ever have it?

Learning to receive isn't that hard. It is about giving yourself an hour or two (even if you have to make an appointment with yourself!) and doing something that brings joy to you. Even if it is something as simple as a walk in the woods, fantastic. Having a massage is wonderfully self-nurturing. Safe touch, relaxing completely with the focus on you for a change. Sitting by a creek with the water flowing and the sun reflecting off the water can be extremely nurturing. Feed the ducks or the fish while you are there. Let yourself merge in nature or in the dark or in the sun. An intimate discussion with a friend, your favorite movie, a special dinner that someone else makes and does the dishes too, the play-offs of your favorite team, time to tinker in your workshop to create that thing you have imagined for years . . .

it doesn't matter—do it and just feel. That feeling is a spark of the very passion you seek.

Find reasons to laugh. Laugh for no reason at all. If you are laughing believe it or not you are almost there.

Passion is laughter that has become systemic.

It is all through your body, mind, and soul. Passion is like that. Passion fills every molecule of every cell in your body with definite direction or an etheric pause, if that is what is needed.

Do you have to have something to be passionate about? Honestly, no. Passion is a state of being, not something to do. If you let your guard down and stop defending yourself, let the tension ooze out of your body, what you will find is the capacity to feel much more deeply than you knew you were capable of.

If you feel that your passion needs direction, what is it that you have always wanted to do but have not ever done? Do *that*. Do something exotic like a hot air balloon ride or a midnight sail. Why save a bucket list for some other day? Do it now!

If you do what you love you will love what you do!

Exercise:
Find Your Heart and Open It!

Physically or mentally take yourself to your favorite place. What is it that you love about that place? It is there that you are able to relax and let go of stress? Are there things there that you love to do even if that means doing nothing? Let yourself sink into that place.

Next, close your eyes. Go back in time. Think of instances when your heart was full. When your child was born, or before that, how you felt with your first love, anything that brought that feeling of swelling into your heart and soul.

Bring that feeling forward into this now. And as you do, breathe deeply and intentionally, allowing your heart space to swell fully. As you exhale, let go of the tension that had guarded your heart.

Maintain the feeling that you have found buried in your being. Breathe again, locking that feeling into your very being.

When you find yourself raising your guard, losing your focus on self, bring your attention back to your heart and breathe that feeling back into place. Carry this feeling into everything that you do.

Chapter 6

Question Everything
(You Don't Know As Much As You Think You Do!)

There is a lot of misinformation out there.
The question is: what applies to us,
and how do we know it's true?

One thing that gets us into trouble time and again is ignoring the obvious. We don't ask enough questions. Sometimes asking questions can feel risky. Why rock the boat, right? We have been conditioned to be accepting of what we don't understand, and in that process we have been rendered powerless. In the meantime, others have gone about creating great successes for themselves because they not only asked the questions, they acted on the answers—and there we are, left behind in their dust.

No don't misinterpret what I am saying here . . . getting trapped in an analytical pattern in which you become lost and even more unaware can be equally as disabling. What it does mean is to be intentionally aware, asking the questions that you need to fully comprehend any situation or questions you have about anything—and then not hesitating to act on what you find.

Having questions is about learning, not about having answers and not about judging. It doesn't matter that we needed to know. Seeking personal expansion is not only okay, it is paramount to a full life! What really matters is what we do with that moment.

Becoming the Conscious Observer

Earlier I wrote about becoming a conscious observer. If we are to live intentionally and to be what we intend, don't you think we have a responsibility to know what we are really experiencing, what people are really saying, and what the real dynamics are in our interactions with others?

Being a conscious observer does not mean setting aside your emotions and looking at the world from the perspective of a drone. What it means is to observe from a step back, noticing what is going on without getting snared in other people's issues or into the drama of a given situation.

Often people are not really saying what they mean, but we believe them because they said so. Later we find out they didn't mean a word of it, they were only making words to please us (or themselves) in the moment. Their actions speak volumes different from their words.

If we had been consciously observing in the first place, we would have seen that perhaps they didn't meet our eyes directly, their body language was saying the complete opposite of what they said—like when they made a promise to us they turned their bodies away from us. Clear signs they weren't telling the truth or didn't really mean what they said at all. But we heard what we wanted to hear and now we are in a situation that is not okay.

How about the times we have reacted with anger, flaunting our temper and being defensive . . . when it wasn't even necessary or appropriate? Maybe saw or heard something and made too quick an assumption, reacting badly only to be very sorry later.

Being a conscious observer is stepping out
of our reflexive, guarded behaviors
into a place of calm observation.

This takes practice. Our tendency is to react reflexively based on our past experiences, but let's be honest—we aren't where we want to be. Time to change our interactions to those of power and truth.

When we allow ourselves to observe without prejudice we begin to experience the truth no matter what.

Time and again it is our predisposed assumptions and our neediness that gets us what we don't want. If we can watch with a new set of eyes and really see what is happening, we will find out that not everyone is as honest as we would like to think. Not everyone means what they say.

Conversely, there are a lot of people we never gave a chance because there was something about them we didn't like. Chances are good they were a lot like some part of us that we don't like, or that feels unsafe to explore, so not wanting to look at that we blew them off.

As we observe with our new eyes we also become more present. Remember, being now is a huge leap toward our new life. We begin to see new and exciting opportunities and avoid the pitfalls of going down a deceptive road. The possibilities of each situation blossom into realities because we were paying enough attention to act on them as they were revealed.

Learning to Be Discerning

Discernment, what a concept. You mean we have the right to decide what is good for us? You bet! Not only the right, but the responsibility. When we discern for ourselves, what we are really doing is choosing whether or not information, a situation, an idea, even a social norm fits us and our needs.

There are a lot of people in our world who will sell us a bill of goods in a heartbeat. There is a lot of misinformation out there. The question is: What applies to us, and how do we know?

Discernment may seem difficult at first because the old habit of lying to ourselves may creep in. So often we find ourselves wanting to believe what we are seeing or hearing because the way we are seeing it is the way we want things to be. We want someone to give us the answers to life, we want someone to tell us how to make things easier, and so when we listen to them that is what we hear.

We lie to ourselves, brushing off the obvious with a lame excuse about why we are right. We see someone who is clean, well dressed, and purported to be an authority on a particular subject and we take their words as gospel, spend our days trying to be who they told us we are, only to find out that their ideas of how we should live our lives are far from anything we ever really wanted. Those ideas worked for that person but are certainly not for us.

On the flip side, we are suspicious of everything and everyone because we don't know how to trust others. We are afraid to trust. So we discount our experiences as a bunch of hooey and go about what we do know, missing a golden opportunity because we reacted a little too quickly.

If we learn to be discerning, to observe consciously and intentionally without jumping to action or conclusions, we begin to experience the honesty we wish to create.

There are a few great questions that you can ask yourself to give yourself a reality check. The first one is:

- How do I really feel about this?

    Taking the time to listen to your body can save you a lot of grief later. Is something nagging at you that you just can't put your finger on? Trust it, and act accordingly!

- Is this the truth?

    Check your honesty. Ask yourself if you are telling yourself the truth or if it's just what you want to hear. This is vital to an acceptable outcome.

- Is this mine, or someone else's?

    This question alone can save you years of grief. Often we take on the feelings or problems of others because that is how we allow ourselves to be set up in a given situation, especially situations that sizzle with differences or high emotions. Make sure the situation or feeling you are about to address is even yours. After a little practice you will find that you were reactive to many situations that weren't even yours to start with!

    We tend to want to fix things, to not have conflict in our experiences, so we start fixing. Or we take on guilt, anger, or other negative emotions that really weren't how we started out feeling at all. If you find yourself becoming agitated in any situation as you observe, ask if what you are feeling is yours. Then be truthful. Sometimes someone is mirroring to you and your buttons are being pushed. If that is the case, own it and then set it aside for now, until you can look at the issue clearly and uninfluenced by others.

- Is action from me required?

  Is what you are noticing in your conscious observation pulling at you to act in some way? Do you want to jump into something because you are excited? Or the opposite, do you want to run because the situation is making you uncomfortable?

  Have a look at your inclinations. Should you really jump into this? Do you know enough to make sure the pool is full of water so that when you leap in you don't hit concrete? Do you really have enough information to act?

  Are you uncomfortable because you haven't been honest with yourself or because the situation really isn't good for you? Once you have honestly considered, choose to act or not.

- What is my responsibility in this, if any?

  Often we feel responsible to act on the behalf of others or to react out of guilt or a sense of responsibility. You are now officially off the hook.

Responsibility is a choice, not an obligation. Whatever you choose, do it because it is really what you want, not what you should want. If you find that you are telling yourself you *should* do something, have a serious look at why you are doing it at all.

Exercise:
Five Questions

Think of three recent situations in which things turned out not to be what you thought. Look at one situation at a time, and discern how you could have acted differently or chosen to react in a way that had a greater benefit for you. As you look at each situation, ask yourself the five questions in this chapter. Answer yourself honestly. You will find that your perception changes greatly based on the questions.

- How do I really feel about this?
- Is this the truth?
- Is this mine, or someone else's?
- Is action from me required?
- What is my responsibility in this, if at all?

Chapter 7

Be What You Mean
(Who Have You Been Kidding, Anyway?)

Look in the mirror. Who do you see? Your Mom?
Your Dad? A grandparent perhaps?
The culmination of criticisms, yours and everyone
else's? A perfect stranger? Look further.

We often slog along in our lives trying to "heal" ourselves, to become some idealistic version of a human being, reading self-help books, following certain behavioral protocol that is supposed to optimize our experiences, taking workshops, going to lectures, buying gadgets and products that are purported to change our lives—but do we really know who we are or what we are trying to accomplish with all that grueling effort? Who is it that we mean to be, and more importantly, how will we feel when we get there?

Do we have to suffer our past miseries to be who we want to be? Do we have to participate with others in their drama and trauma to get to the place we mean to go? Are we who other people say we are? No! No! and No!

How can we shake loose all the things that are really holding us down? How do we find those issues so we can realize them in the first place? This chapter is about realizing a definite direction, and how to be what we mean with ease.

Even though we are intrinsically perfect and magnificent beings of creation, what we believe has everything to do with who we are. If we see ourselves as less than perfect, it must be so. If we see ourselves in need of, we must be. If we see ourselves as unsatisfied, we feel unfulfilled. If we believe that we lack, then we do.

Look in the mirror. Who do you see? Your Mom? Your Dad? A grandparent perhaps? The culmination of yours and everyone else's criticisms? Look further. Meet your eyes in the mirror. Beyond the physical, who is looking back at you? You are.

A soul embodied and incarnated for an experience of L.I.F.E.

But we believe differently, so we don't see, feel, or experience our excellence. We know we want things to change but we feel stuck or don't know how to get things moving in a different direction. Changing our lives is as easy as changing our minds. Perspective is everything.

Perceptions are an imaging system that human beings utilize in such a way as to define experience. In order to change the experience, one has only to change the perception. In other words, how we see and believe our experiences determines the reality that we live. All we must do to change our reality is to change how we see it.

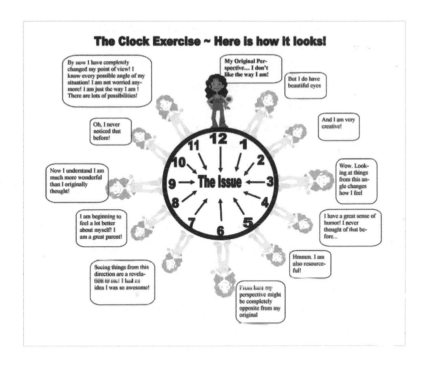

The Clock Exercise ~ Here is how it looks!

In order to be who we want to be, we must change our belief systems. An easy way to do this is to picture the face of a clock with all the numbers present. Picture yourself in the middle of the clock, where the hands are connected. The twelve-o'clock mark represents your current perspective of yourself in the center of the clock face—everything you believe about yourself in this now.

Absorb what you believe about yourself. Once you have a good understanding of your present view, imagine stepping over to the one-o'clock position. From this perspective, your point of view changes. See yourself from a different angle. If you believed that your body was imperfect, see now how beautiful your fingers or your eyes are. Absorb this new perspective.

Then imagine moving over to the two-o'clock position. See yourself again through new eyes. If you thought that you were perhaps not a success, begin to look at the moments in your life that you were a success.

Continue around the face of the clock. With each station, find a different way to see yourself. Some of the things that you see may not be what you would consider positive. Take note of those things and have a look at them from another perspective or number on the clock. How can you change your point of view so that you see yourself differently?

This wonderful exercise can be used for any subject. You can even make a clock on the driveway with chalk, or in the yard or living room with whatever you have handy. Always start at twelve o'clock to begin your explorative journey.

When faced with tough or even everyday decisions it is always a great idea to use this process or one like it to weigh out consequences before jumping into action. To learn to see all sides of yourself and your life as well as the issues that come up takes away the feelings of panic or inadequacy that often occur. You are no longer acting reflexively but instead from a balanced, secure perspective.

Other People's Stuff

When we look in the mirror what we see is often what others have told us or implied. Just because others express opinions or make requirements of us *does not* mean they are right or what they say or believe is true.

What you know is truth. What you remember is the extension of that truth beyond measurable limits. No one else's truth lives your life for you.

That we use others to model ourselves is a terrible disservice to the real us who is clawing to come out! But we do. Over and over again . . . "How do I look?" "Did I do a good job?" "What should I do about . . . ?" "What do you think about . . . ?" "Did you hear about . . . ? It could have been us." And on we go, begging for validation, feeling the need to have someone else approve of who we are.

And let's be honest here. Everyone who tells us anything is doing so from a perspective they have developed over their lifetime. That perspective may or may not be particularly functional or even healthy.

Yet we want so badly to see ourselves looking terrific in other people's eyes. Generally, what people mirror to us is what we don't want to see. For instance, we see a trait that we loathe in someone. It bothers us so much that we get off-the-wall mad—even if that person is a perfect stranger.

The truth is, if we were really being honest what we would see was that maybe we had a little bit or a great deal of the same trait, we just didn't want to admit it. It is easier to project our beliefs outward to others and blame them. The problem is that they are only as aware of themselves as they choose to be, or have the life skills to realize deeper awareness.

So, here we are, looking to others to be our mirror, to reinforce our confidence, to know who we are and what we are about, what we should do and even how to do it, not realizing that they don't have a clue who they are, what they are doing, or even how to gauge themselves any better than we do! But sure, they all have opinions . . . Geez. *What are we thinking?*

Okay. From now on you are off the hook. You don't have to care at all what anyone else thinks, says, or does. You need only to look inside from whatever perspective you want, and you decide what your experience is, what you will do and who you are. When you can do that you can begin to be free.

No More Worries

When we aren't afraid anymore and we don't need anyone else's opinion about anything we begin to feel glimpses of freedom inside us. We begin to act from a less convoluted perspective, one that is ours entirely and dependent upon no other influences.

Now, what is there to worry about, really?

> Worrying is like leaning out in front of yourself
> looking for trouble that doesn't exist.

Since you no longer need to care what anyone else thinks, says, or does, this means you also no longer need anyone else's approval. It also means that if people do have judgments about you, they are coming from their stuff, not yours.

So, when others try to bait you, to draw you into the illusion of imperfection, you don't have to go there. You don't have to believe them because you are none of that!

As you perfect this new point of view, an amazing thing begins to happen. You become authentic. You are no longer afraid. Your vulnerabilities are no longer your enemy. No one else's opinion matters. You no longer need to compare yourself to others. You . . . are . . . becoming . . . *you!*

Exercise:
Take a Walk with a Different Set of Ears

From your new set of perspectives, take a walk downtown, in the mall, at the ball field, wherever there are a lot of people. Listen to your inner thoughts as you walk. Where is your attention? Observe yourself as you move through the crowd.

Can you catch yourself being judgmental? Comparing your outfit to what someone else is wearing, or thinking, *look how that person is acting*? Really pay attention. Be the conscious observer. Remember that if others' opinions about you don't matter, neither do your opinions of them!

Chapter 8

Have a Sense of Humor
(When Did Life Get So Serious? Laugh!)

*Being serious about everything is against our nature.
We have to laugh. We must laugh!*

Oh, do we ever need to laugh! But we don't do it enough. We spend so much time all tied up, not letting our true feelings out. Laughter literally releases body chemicals that are great for our health and well-being. So why are we frowning? Why are we so tight? Does life have to be so doggone serious all of the time?

We are still protecting our inner child, one who is historic, but still whining in the background. How do we comfort that child, and how do we break free from subconscious immaturity once and for all?

One of the attributes we gain as we mature is a sense of responsibility to ourselves and others. We are given the instruction and impression that responsibility takes a certain appearance, and that if we are not responsible, we are failures. As we become more and more responsible, we begin to lose our innocence.

Amber Alert! Help! I've Lost My Inner Child!

About the time we enter puberty, maybe even a little sooner than that, we begin to notice what everyone else thinks of us. Recognizing what others (particularly our peers) think of us becomes one of the most important aspects of our development. Their views of us become our focus, their approval our goal, and those opinions affect our general perception of our self. Our innocent sense of self begins to fade, and we want to be all grown up.

We begin to dress and act according to what is acceptable in our peer group. We begin to talk like our friends, using inflections, expressions, and phrases so that we fit in. We begin to wean ourselves from our families to a large degree, and at the same time, more and more demands are made of us. We are becoming older and therefore must assume more responsibilities. More expectations are made of us, and consequences generally follow if we don't meet those expectations.

Later we are required to find a job, some kind of work to contribute to our growing expenses and wants. Our jobs have further requirements, and our time begins to belong less and less to us.

Some of us continue our educations and move away from home to go to college. There, we must meet grade-point requirements; we are tested in a pass-or-fail manner. We are expected to choose a field of study—what we want to do for the rest of our lives—at a young age. We have to make lifelong commitments to things we aren't yet even familiar with, let alone passionate about.

In the process of all of these changes come relationships and ultimately a love with whom we may even create a family. That family needs to be supported, and we are the breadwinners.

We go to work, we come home, and everyone has needs and demands. We lose touch with our inner selves and often give up altogether on our passions because we don't have the energy or there just isn't enough time.

The lives we had so looked forward to become a conforming blur of everyone else's needs, wants, and desires, and there always doesn't seem to be room for extracurricular activities that we love or want to do. What a gruesome picture! The lives that we so anticipated and the milestones that we wanted to achieve ultimately are set aside while we wear the albatross of responsibility around our necks.

Lighten Up!

We *have* to laugh. We *must* laugh! Being serious about everything is against our nature. When we don't laugh, it is because we are guarded. We have built defensive walls all around us. To some people, laughter is considered silliness or even a weakness. These perceptions come from the same perspective that prompted us to guard ourselves in the first place. To others, laughter means emotional exposure. If you find something funny or humorous, you might be showing too much of your private self.

The truth is that the more we laugh, the more we are willing to come out and play, the more balanced we become. This doesn't mean we have to shirk our responsibilities. We just need to take a different perspective about ourselves and our place in our world.

We have to lighten up!

It isn't as hard as you might think. How many times have you nearly busted a gut trying not to laugh because you thought laughing wasn't appropriate at the time? Laughter is a release mechanism that reduces stress and tension and allows us to be authentic. The truth is that when we don't laugh, when we hold it inside in the name of being appropriate, all of those feelings will come out in the form of hysteria at the wrong time.

I remember being a young adult and carrying my guardedness around like a trophy. I was determined to be the strong one, to fit in and be everything that was expected of me. I thought I was impenetrable. Everyone thought I was so tough when on the inside I was a marshmallow. I was in great need of emotional support, but I had little to none. Being that protected all the time was hard work, and I wasn't particularly happy in general.

My brother was engaged to an extremely volatile woman, and I knew the match would never last. My son had been requested to be the ring bearer in his uncle's wedding. He was just a little guy, maybe three or four years old.

The morning of the wedding, as the bride was getting ready, she was an absolute terror, Bridezilla to the max. She was screaming profanities and yelling at everyone in her presence. By God, it was all about her, and she made sure everyone got that point. She had an idea of just how her wedding was going to be, and she was determined to have that vision at everyone else's expense. One particular point of tension for her was that her veil wasn't staying put. She had been to the hairdresser, and whatever had been put in her hair had made it so silky that the comb of her long veil kept sliding off. That her veil seating was precarious made her even more aggressive with everyone. Her behavior was so raw that it was painful to be around, and I ultimately left the room.

The bride finally seemed to have everything put together, and the wedding began. There they were, the bride, my brother, the attendants, and my little guy, who stood right next to the bride with his tiny pillow, proudly holding the soon-to-be-worn rings. He was so cute in his little tuxedo and was very proud to have such a responsibility. Partway through the ceremony, my son wanted to say something to the bride.

So he began to tug on her veil. It was all he could reach.

All I could think of was how she was going to lose it if her veil came off. It was an extremely tense moment. Hell-bound for hysteria, I started to laugh. God, I tried so hard to hold it in. And the more I tried to stifle myself, the more I laughed. I became hysterical, laughing so hard I was crying. In a vain effort to become invisible in my uncontrolled laughter, I literally lay down between church pews. And I still couldn't stop.

And my son tugged on the veil harder. Oh God.

My laughter was contagious. Several people around me saw what was going on, and they started to laugh at me. What was I going to do? Ruin my brother's wedding? I was sitting in the very front of the church, so leaving while I was cracking up wasn't really an option.

Well, I just couldn't help it. I laughed until I cried. And the more I realized I was out of control, the more I laughed. I was so embarrassed, but I just couldn't stop laughing. Somehow, in spite of me, the wedding took place, the rings made it onto their respective fingers, and no, the veil didn't come off, although to this day I don't know how.

Looking back, I realize now that that moment was a trigger for me to let out years of frustration at trying to hide my true feelings. In what seemed like an interminable few minutes, my body had released more chemicals, had released more pressure, than I knew I had. What a relief!

Then I had to beat myself up for being so inappropriate. But after I got over myself, I was able to laugh about it. I still do. Somehow, contrary to all my fears of dire consequences, no one ever said a word! My fear of repercussions was all in my imagination. It was as if my laughing bout had been invisible and inaudible. Everyone was so caught up in the wedding that I had gone entirely unnoticed except to a few people around me who had great senses of humor!

Allowing ourselves to become bottled up emotionally only serves to create an emotional pressure cooker that, sooner or later, has to blow if we don't take the lid off. When we are self-defended and don't laugh, soon we feel we are unfulfilled. We begin to feel spiritually and emotionally empty. We look to others to fill this place inside us, or we try to fill it with stuff of a material nature. None of this helps, but we keep doing it. And we teach our kids to hold it all in. Is that what we want for them?

Letting our emotions flow isn't as hard as we think. To do so, we must simply return to our innocence. The child within us is anxiously waiting to come out. Inside, each of us wants to come out and be free.

Getting beyond Serious

Beginning our journey back to inner freedom requires us only to get in touch with the child within us. For some of us, that child may seem to be flailing, unsupported, abandoned, unloved, or, worse, even abused. Even if that is true, the child within us can learn to feel safe and free. We are that child, and we do know what we want, what we need, but we have denied ourselves these things for what seems like forever.

So maybe as kids we really didn't have what we needed emotionally. Or at least we perceive that we didn't. That was then. Now we can choose our experiences. The question is, what do we need now, and why aren't we getting it? We can't look to someone else for our laughter or for our inner freedom. We must stop seeing ourselves as wounded or broken, and instead take on the new perception that we are perfect in every moment.

When we hold in our emotions, one of the first things to happen is that we stop breathing, literally. Our bodies become tense, and for a moment we are paralyzed in our existence until we take our next breath. A great way to move past these kinds of moments is first to become aware of them and second to take an intentional ten or twelve deep breaths several times a day to relieve our tension. Breathing also helps keep our energy, or chi, flowing more freely.

If, as we breathe, we can also imagine the child within us and all of its emotions, we can direct our breath to our inner child, nurturing it. As we breathe life back into our inner child, we can allow our hearts to expand and begin to love that child fully and unconditionally, the way it always wanted to be loved.

As we become more and more aware of the feelings of our inner child, we become more aware of just how guarded we became and even perhaps what it was we were defending. We find basic, raw emotions born in the heart of our inner child. Oh, how we needed! And who noticed? We did.

Awareness is the key to relaxing in ourselves.

Awareness creates perceptions. What we perceive is based on our awareness of the now in combination with our history. Our egos become involved, trying at once to bolster our opinions of self and at the same time destroying who we think we are. So let's move past our ego.

Our general reaction to the demands of life is to buck up and do our best to win approval. It happens at work a lot. The boss comes along and drops a bomb in our laps in the form of a project that needs to be completed within a ridiculous timeline. It is an inconvenient and nearly impossible task, but we are so grateful to have been noticed that, after an initial hesitation, about a split second, we gratefully accept the responsibility and immediately go about doing the best job ever—even though that means working day and night for perhaps weeks. On the due date, we confidently march into the boss's office with the completed project in hand. It is the best work we have ever done. Instead of getting the kudos that we secretly expect, we barely get a nod of recognition. We feel let down and empty. But then, this isn't the first time.

The child within us is devastated, and so we continue to try harder. The problem is that all of that trying is really at our expense. No one else really notices or even cares, or if they do, they may be jealous and accuse us of being the favorite or a brown-noser. Geez!

In the same vein, our children work very hard to get our attention, our praise, and to know that they are loved completely. They compete with their siblings for more attention from us. Ultimately, there is an argument between our children that we are then expected to moderate, or we correct what seems to be inappropriate behavior, and our children's secret fears that we don't love them enough has been validated, even though they created the situation.

When we are kids, we develop patterns like this as we do our best to become noticed, validated, and, yes, even loved. These patterns carry into our adult lives much like the example above, yet somehow we never seem to get what we want or need. That is because we are looking to others to fulfill us.

In order to find our senses of humor again, we must become present with ourselves, get fully into our bodies. As we do, we can become aware of the moments that our bodies tense up and we stop breathing. These physical reactions are huge clues that in this moment we are defending ourselves. From what? Why?

Well, the reasons really don't matter. What does is finding compassion for ourselves. And then laughing about how serious we think we are. And then laughing again and again, releasing of a lifetime of tension in this beautiful way.

What is it that you dreamed of as a child? What were your favorite activities? What brought you a feeling of empowerment? What were your favorite activities? Games? TV shows? Movies?

Do those things again. Take yourself back to your fantasy worlds. Touch the freedom of those moments. Buy a kite. Blow some bubbles and watch them reach the sky. Imagine yourself riding one all the way to the heavens. Get a can of Silly String and ambush someone. (Make sure you have a can ready for them as well!) Stomp in a mud puddle with both feet. (I did that recently and shocked everyone present. Their eyes got big, and no one knew how to respond. I laughed like a little kid, quite contrary to most everyone's perception of me. . . . It was fantastic!)

Whatever it takes, let your inner child be free.

Your inner child isn't subject to anyone's approval but yours. Most of all, instead of putting yourself down when you feel you've screwed up, laugh, laugh, laugh. The mistake doesn't matter to anyone but you.

Exercise:
Come Out to Play

Think back to how you played as a child. Do that. Invite some friends if you want. Get a game of Twister and a couple of pizzas and have a slumber party, pajamas and all. Buy a quart of bubbles and go outside and ride your imagination away with each tenuous orb. Buy a couple dozen cans of Silly String and start a string war. Play Jacks. Have a scavenger hunt, play hide and seek. Do whatever you loved to do when you were small. Whatever you choose may feel silly at first. You will find that you are stiff inside yourself. Relax. Have fun. How much fun you have is always and entirely up to you.

Practice laughing even if you are alone. Laugh out loud. From your belly. At anything and at everything. Release your inhibitions and begin to feel the rhythm of your true emotions.

Chapter 9

Change Is Magnificent
(Stop Resisting!)

*Change is an expression of our willingness
to live to our fullest potential.
Change is the impetus to wider experience
and greater depth of feeling.
Change is necessary if we are to break out
of our complacency and step boldly into our lives
and all that they may bring.
Change may seem terrifying but it doesn't have to be.*

The first thing we do when faced with the possibility of change is to kick and scream and resist like a coyote caught in a snare. We fight, we howl, but the inevitable change comes anyway and there we are suffocating in our resistance. The more we refuse to give in to change, the more stagnant and even difficult our experience of life becomes.

Stagnancy leads to resignation and resignation leads to surrender. Surrender to the idea that we have been dealt a lot in life and that is all we get. And there we sit.

If we put a voice to our resistance it would sound something like this: "Oh poor me. I am not willing to change a thing. I am afraid of what I don't understand. If I allow change then I am not in control anymore. I am not budging! Why oh why don't I get what I want just the way I am?"

Oh, brother. Want a little cheese with that whine? As if we are ever in control anyway. Hard to have sympathy for an attitude like that, yet how many of us really do have that mind-set? The truth is that just the way we are is magnificent. It is how we perceive ourselves that has everything to do with who we are.

What we know, what is familiar is our safety zone. It is, as we discussed earlier, often our comfortable discomfort. The only way to truly leave that zone is for change to occur. Even if that change is only within us, that is the greatest change of all.

Change is a choice. Sometimes, though, change carries us through no apparent initiative of our own. Sometimes when we have resisted long enough, unmoving, seemingly uninvited change comes in like a north wind, clearing everything that is an obstacle to our growth and taking us expediently to entirely new circumstances that are unfamiliar and require us to alter our previous habits and thinking.

Change forces choice, but change is a choice. You have the power to change your existence right now. There is no change without chaos. There is no chaos without a catalyst. You are the catalyst. And the result of chaos is . . . magnificence!

Miracles Happen When We Are Open to Change

A miracle is an event or action that is amazing, extraordinary, or unexpected. A miracle may seem contrary to the laws of nature or to be an act of God.

Miracles are happening all around us in every moment of every day. They are the little surprises we get when we least expect them. Or maybe, when we are feeling down, at the perfect time someone tells us how amazingly perfect we are. When we are out of money and wondering how to make ends meet, and we get a check in the mail that we didn't even know was coming. There are all kinds of miracles, like when our children say their first words or take their first steps. When we say the absolute right thing to the right person in the right moment, and an opportunity we didn't expect reveals itself, like a new job, or how to fix something, or something we really, really needed to know but didn't know where to look for. Miracles come in every form and size. Don't be so busy looking for the big booming voice of God that you miss the little miracles all around you!

When we have resisted ourselves long enough, the very change we have resisted comes anyway, and sometimes in a much more difficult way than if we had been more open to it earlier. Some part of us deep down is screaming for our lives to be more colorful, complete, and fulfilled. As we discussed earlier, creation is listening, and it brings us exactly what we request, even when we don't expect it.

For example: Day after day we go to the same job, hating it. We are bored, unfulfilled, unchallenged, and yet every morning we get up and go again. After all, we need that money, right? We do the bare minimum to get through the day or, conversely, work way too hard in order to please the boss because that gives us value, right? (Wrong!)

One morning we get to work and as we walk through the office people step back like Moses parting the Red Sea. Through the chasm of people we see The Boss standing there waiting for us. Uh-oh.

The boss tells us our services are no longer needed. No muss, no fuss, just pack up and go on home. Shocked, devastated, hurt, we pack our box or two and head to the car. We put the boxes in the back seat and get into the driver's seat. Confusion sets in. Where do we go now? What are we going to do? Oh God, now what?

There are a lot of us who, in that moment, would go home and have a humongous pity party. Our livelihood is lost. We might even panic.

But, there is another way to handle this. First of all, we must know that there is a reason for everything and for everything there is a reason. Let's admit it. We were bored, unsatisfied, and unchallenged. We really wanted something different. We got it.

So let's take a ride. After we leave the office, we drive down the road and shortly we come to a stoplight. Usually we wouldn't turn here at all, but something inside us says to turn right here right now . . . Okay, what the heck, we aren't on the clock anymore, so we turn. As we go down the lane, a big red ball rolls out in front of us followed by a very excited pooch. We hit the brakes and come to a stop just as the dog runs in front of us. Darn dog.

While we are stopped waiting for the dog and his ball to get out of the way, a man walks up and thanks us for stopping. "Sorry about that. He got out the door faster than I could stop him"—and he notices our boxes . . . "Hey—are you moving?"

"No. I just got laid off of my job. I don't know what I am going to do now."

"Well, what kind of work do you do?"

Now here is a pivotal moment. Do we say what we were doing or what we really want to do?

Absolutely hands down—what we want.

"Well, I was repairing computers, but the truth is that over all these years I have had some outstanding ideas for products that would enhance the computer industry by a long shot. I have even built some prototypes. This is my passion and one day I hope to put my creative ideas to work . . ."

The man gets a peculiar look on his face and briefly pauses. Then, he sticks his hand out and says, "Hi. I am Peter Gabriel, CEO of CreativeElectronics.com. You know, we have a place in our company for creative people like you. Why don't you come by the office, say, around two this afternoon, and we will talk? If, of course, you are interested . . ."

Flabbergasted, all we can muster is an incredulous, "Sure . . . okay . . . thanks . . ."

At two we go to the office to meet Mr. Gabriel and he shows us around. The entire place is a plethora of creative ideas in motion. The environment is nothing like we have ever seen. Bright, cheerful, comfortable. Everyone seems really happy to be there. This is bizarre, but . . . hmmm . . .

Long story short, Mr. Gabriel, Peter, offers us a job that is three times our previous pay grade with twice the benefits and an open schedule in which we can come and go as necessary. He pays to move us to a different state and provides enough of a sign-on bonus to buy a new home there.

Not only that, but soon after we begin our new job, we become so creative and successful with our ideas that soon we are put in charge of innovative ideas and the technicians who build the prototypes! We win Best of Show for new products at the annual show our first year! And all because we turned right instead of going in a familiar direction!

Magic happens when we are open to the infinite possibilities that are available to us. Change can literally carry us to the door of an entirely new life experience. The key is that we have to be willing to walk through that door when it opens.

Sometimes we open those doors without realizing what we are doing. On other occasions we literally and intentionally open up opportunities for positive change in our lives merely by being totally present in a now—and noticing some subtle clue that an opportunity is at hand and going for it. How we do it doesn't matter. We just have to be willing to step forward into new territory.

With changes come challenges. Of course, like anything else, change comes in degrees. Part of why we see change as so difficult is because we look at the whole picture or set of circumstances as if we have to deal with everything all at once. Remember that everything complex is made up of definable small parts, each with simplicity of existence.

Everything complex is made up of definable small parts, each with simplicity of existence.

And, besides, nothing within you ever changes without your participation.

I remember when I was a kid worrying about something that seemed like a huge dilemma: My dad would ask me how to eat an elephant. My mind would go directly to the literal aspects of eating that elephant: the size and weight of the beast and even the toughness of the skin of an elephant (could my small teeth even bite it?). In my imagination the elephant was covered in mud so it would be way too dirty to eat! I would get crunchy teeth from the dirt!

Nothing within you ever changes without your participation.

About then Dad would laugh and say, "You eat an elephant one bite at a time, of course!"

Change is like eating the elephant. We have to take the first bite, followed by another, then another. Change can seem overwhelming, but if we find ourselves immersed in the unknown all we need to do is begin to unravel the simplicities.

The simplicities are our lifelines
in any set of circumstances.

The simplicities become a trail, a map from one moment to the next. One by one, they unfold to a greater and greater understanding of any experience.

In other words, we often become so overwhelmed by the immensity of a situation that we fail to see that if we just deal with one aspect at a time, before you know, it we have surmounted the entire situation!

For instance, when I was a real estate broker, I volunteered to be in charge of the annual Board of Realtors Christmas banquet. Of course, I never do anything half way, and I wanted to provide the absolute best event this group had ever seen. It was a much bigger deal than I had realized. It involved planning menus, finding entertainment that everyone would enjoy, getting decorations, table settings, renting a place to have the event, and in fact far more details than I could have imagined, but now the event was my responsibility. It had little to no budget, and it required entertainment, a sound system, bar staff, and a whole lot more. When I first sat down to plan the event I was overwhelmed. It was vastly out of my realm of experience. Being a visionary, I tend to see things in a grand way, successful and completed, not all of the little details that get you there. In fact, I abhor details.

The first thing to do was to separate out all of the parts to the event. What were the actual components of this event and what would it require to put them all together? It really didn't take long to divide it all out once I got past my resistance.

I made an outline. To get this, we need that. Okay, now what? Well, I thought, the next thing to do was to find a place that specialized in that kind of event to help with the details (the food, décor, staffing, and so on). So I did. I went over the menus with the facility staff, and I told them how I envisioned the room being set up from what I knew would be happening at the banquet. They decorated around my plans. Because this event was for such a diverse group of people, I chose more than one kind of entertainment. First I chose one that everyone would participate in. With the assistance of another Realtor, I wrote a simple, hilarious play, and we gave everyone their lines to the play as they came in the door. No one knew what came before or after their given lines. It was too funny. We also hired a DJ, who brought a wide variety of music and was open to requests. Yes, you can please almost everyone! The establishment provided bartenders for an extra fee. In order to keep costs down, we required all attendees to bring their own bottles and leave their bottle at the bar with their name on it. One step at a time the pieces of this complex event came together, resulting in a gala that was a smashing success! When it was completed, that elephant didn't look so big at all, and everything came off without a hitch.

What we don't often realize is that all change comes from within. It is not something that happens to us. It is something that on some level we require for the expansion of our soul's experience.

No matter what we say, or what we do or do not do, some part of us deep inside is screaming for us to do something different. Are we listening?

Exercise:
Make a Change Now

Think of one thing that you really want to change in your life. It doesn't have to be the most major change on your list (unless you want it to be). Choose something that for a long time you have said "if only" or "one day I am going to . . ."

Whatever change you choose, make sure that it will take you out of your comfort zone. It can be as easy as changing the hairstyle you have worn for years or the color of your clothes. It can be to rearrange a room that has been the same forever, ending or beginning a relationship, moving house, or reacting to certain people in a new way. Start with something small if necessary.

Oh! Feel that resistance to making it happen? Are the excuses on autopilot, telling you all the reasons you shouldn't change anything? Those excuses are lies that are born of fear.

Even if you don't have a plan, make that change! Do so without any expectations and know that, whatever it is, it will be perfect in its outcome.

Oh, and never look back. What was, has been. You aren't there anymore, remember? The time is now! Go for it.

Chapter 10

Relationships Do Have a Purpose
(What Are We Looking for and What Are We Willing to Give Back?)

We must realize the power of relationships.
No matter what kind they are, they can enhance us
to no end, or be to our detriment.
Every relationship is a mirror to what is happening
inside of us. The question is, can we see that?

Our relationships and the dynamics within them are a direct reflection of who we are inside.

Ouch! That statement may hurt, but it is the truth. All of our relationships mirror to us something about ourselves. Typically we want to blame the other person for the failure or discomfort within our relationships, but the truth is that on some level we are getting exactly what we sought. If we find ourselves fighting to find our value in our relationships, always feeling betrayed or left out, we might consider that we haven't acknowledged our value from the inside out.

How many relationships have *you* had? Have they worked out? If not, why not? What were you looking for in the other person or people? Did not getting it bring you to another, and perhaps even others, so that you were just repeating the same situation time and time again?

What are we looking for? With family? Friends? Lovers? Mates? Why are we not finding it? What kind of dynamics do we bring to our relationships that jeopardize the outcome?

Most of us get into relationships with an agenda. We may not even be aware of what our agenda is, but there it is running our show from the background.

Our neediness—stemming from a sense of insecurity, emotional emptiness, or even sexual desire—puts us in a position of vulnerability that ultimately gets us into trouble. At the very least we become disappointed that our counterparts just don't seem to give us what we need. The truth is that we looked to them to give us what we thought we didn't have. How could they possibly know what to give us if we can't find and acknowledge the lack of it within ourselves? Isn't it time to be finished with neediness? Aren't we ready to embark on entirely new relationship experiences?

Relationships have many faces, but honestly, can all be approached from the same perspective? When we look to another to fill something in us, we have some kind of expectations of what that fulfillment will look like or feel like. As we look to someone else for fulfillment, we lay the potential of our happiness into the laps of our counterparts. *What if* we tried a new approach, like letting everyone, including ourselves, off the hook?

The real secret to a healthy relationship of any kind is to realize that no one has what we are looking for except us.

*If we don't value ourselves, recognizing that we are whole
and perfect beings just as we are, who else is going
to give us that value? We cannot accept from others
what we can't recognize in ourselves!*

Valuing ourselves goes back to acknowledging our perfection. Some may say that recognizing our perfection and hence valuing ourselves is impossible, because others have criticized us for not doing enough or being enough, and thus have taught us to loathe our imperfection. But honestly, those people are passing judgment from their own senses of lack or need.

If we can have relationships that allow for everyone to be who they are, without judgment or fear of reprisal, then we can relax and embrace life to its fullest potential.

Why Love Is Not Like a Hallmark Card

If we go about life thinking that real love is like that depicted in country songs, greeting cards, and romanticized commercials, what we get are either codependent or idealized surface relationships that have no depth or long-term chance for survival. Why? Because most cards, most love songs, most anything related to love that is advertised commercially paints a codependent picture of romance. In other words, "I can't live without you." Basically these kinds of representations give us the example of finding someone we are attracted to, then handing them our power with a big red bow attached. They leave little to no room for the sacredness of self. That is not to say that romance isn't a wonderful thing. It surely is! But let's get real about it.

When we are able to love ourselves unconditionally, accepting ourselves as we are and who we are no matter what, we find inner peace like nothing we have ever experienced. As we find that peace, we begin to emanate it to everyone around us. We have a glow about us that is irresistible to others. People gravitate to us like moths to a flame. We are a flame. We are bright with the secrets of life.

Our vulnerabilities, which are our fears and previous experiences from which our fear originated, hide in our subconscious and dictate how we react to any given situation. Like the exercise we did in chapter 4, Identifying Your Fears, when we have accepted our fears, we are no longer vulnerable to being hurt by others. Our guard is then down, and we become authentic in our relations.

As we learn to become authentic, there is nothing to cover up. Our secrets become moot, and we can be at ease any time, anywhere, with anyone. We become unconditional.

Being unconditional means that we not only accept ourselves for who we are, but we accept everyone else for who they are as well. We become more aware of the motivations of others—what they really mean and even why they mean it. Because we start to really get it, that being authentic is so much easier, and life goes so much more smoothly, we are off the hook, and so are they.

When we find this kind of freedom, we are able to experience our feelings at very deep levels because we are no longer hiding from them. And because we are able to feel so deeply, we also become able to give our love more freely. No more withholding. No more guarding our perceived imperfections and pain. Instead, we find only purity of relations on authentic levels.

This is true love. First loving the self, and then loving others, becomes unconditional and can be done with ease and grace. The freedom of this is incomparable.

Real love is not a romantic idealistic fantasy. It is a state of being. When we love ourselves, and we live each moment from that complete self-acceptance, others love us back. When we love ourselves, we find it much easier to have compassion for others. In fact, when we *are* love, we are able to see ourselves in the eyes of everyone we meet. When we find unconditionality in ourselves, we are able to see much more clearly, because nothing is a threat to us, and those things that we previously saw as challenges now appear to be opportunities.

Finding Fulfillment from the Inside Out

Finding fulfillment on our own isn't really that hard. It begins with self-acknowledgment. Fulfillment from the inside out is nothing more than changing our perception of self. When we do, the entire world looks different to us. Gone are the negativities that haunted our days. Gone is the pain of victimhood. Gone is the angst over if or when we will be loved. What is left is the opportunity for pure joy in life.

As you read this, I imagine at this point you are saying, "Yes, but . . ." Or, "What if so-and-so won't go along with this new me?" Or, "That sounds way too hard." Or, "My relationship may not be perfect, but . . ."

There are any number of defensive responses you may have to this information. Look at them. These are part of your defense filters that keep you rooted in place, unable to move forward into greater and different relationships.

Taking responsibility for our experiences and removing the blame from others is a huge step toward having what we want. Typically we tend to want to blame others for not being who or what we thought we had in them. The truth is that those people did the best they could—or not. The point is that it really doesn't matter. The question is, did we do the best we could, and did we learn anything? Or are we going to choose to suffer, wallowing in our pain, carrying that previous relationship around like a dead animal?

When we cart the past around with us, we leave no room for what we really want now.

Worse, we inflict our pain from previous experiences onto the next unsuspecting victim that we befriend or fall in love with, treating them as if they are the one who injured us in the first place. How on earth is this new person supposed to stand a chance? The child within us is mad, hurt, frustrated, and looking for someone to fix us and make it right. It ain't gonna happen.

First of all, no one is a mind reader. How can the new relation possibly know what's up when they weren't there previously and so aren't even aware of the experience that we had? They can't! Yet we expect that either they will fix what is broken or they will fill the perceived gap we think someone else left in us. And that gap is filled with pain. There is no room for anything else and no way to experience unconditionality, that is for sure!

> The truth is that the pain is our chosen path.
> If we want something different,
> all we have to do is choose differently.

But first we have to get right with ourselves. Let's admit our part of our experiences. After all, they are our experiences. We chose, we reacted, and we acted. Now let's get real and get into a healthier mode.

There Are No Mistakes

People come together for great purposes. Sometimes we know why, but more often than not we never know. In fact, coming together is perfection personified.

I used to say that the reason relationships didn't succeed was that people just didn't try hard enough. What I have learned—

what I know—is that often relationships end because people *do* try too hard, for whatever reason. They do so from within their private agenda, which isn't always on the forefront of their awareness.

Sometimes though, relationships just run their course and finish. Sometimes they finish with grace and ease, but more often they end with one or more of the participants being hurt and/or angry. But there aren't any mistakes in why or how we come together with others.

In the grand scheme of things, we are part of an intricate weaving of souls, having simple yet complex relations with others as we are infinitely choreographed to do. Sometimes a relationship is a flash in the pan. Others are for lifetimes. Each has purpose and opportunity, and it is up to us what we do with that.

Sometimes relationships are Karmic. This word is really overused, but in this case it is highly applicable. Karma is simply a repeating pattern that requires new awareness or action. It will occur over and over again until we choose differently or come to a realization that things don't have to be that way and we stop it. Once we choose or act differently in that repeated kind of situation, we change or end that Karma and the pattern will stop.

For instance, karmically speaking, maybe there are things that we can do together with the other person that we couldn't accomplish for ourselves. We harmonize in a perfect creation of relationship and events. With the energy and aid of another person, things set up perfectly for us to accomplish life lessons or growth or even setbacks (as we see them), so that we can become more aware within the journey of our souls. At the same time, we are contributing to the journey of the other person as well, and, for both of us, the Karmic pattern completes.

More often than not there comes a time in Karmic relationships when these influences are finished and the reasons for the relationship are completed. In this type of situation, the relationship decays and separation occurs. It is a universal happening. That doesn't mean anyone is at fault. Sometimes we are complete in a relationship and it serves us both to go on to whatever is next for each of us. No one has to be right or wrong. Simply put, the job is done, so we go on to what is next. This doesn't mean that the relationship wasn't important or was less valuable than others. In fact, Karmic relationships can be some of the most powerful and satisfying or challenging that we can have.

Our greatest love, whether or not we are still with that person, was no mistake. No matter how it turned out, that love took us to our first human depths and heights of loving another person in such a way. We know what that feels like and don't have to grieve it if it is gone; we need only to know that we are capable of feeling great love at *any time.*

Our most painful relationship wasn't an error of God or anyone else either. It was an opportunity for us to expand to new and different awareness, and to make different choices than we had before. Unfortunately, perhaps, part of that learning curve didn't feel so good because, instead of getting the message, we resisted, thinking that the other person had something we needed, and the relationship became so dysfunctional that it was very painful. The question remains: Did we get the message, or are we still going to have to go through the same lesson again and again until we learn something different?

If we are open and choose to see, every one of our relationships teaches us something. The real question is: Are we ready to learn? Or do we just want to feel sorry for ourselves because we don't think we got what we wanted or needed? Our painful relationships are generally caused by our fighting against our own fears. Sometimes that comes from projecting our needs onto someone else who can't possibly fulfill what they don't understand. Or maybe we are simply mismatched. Often we attract exactly the person we need so that we can choose to change a path of behavior or learn to greater depths, but we don't see it that way. We make our misery entirely the other person's fault.

Painful relationships, when there is arguing, abuse, dissonance, or other seemingly negative forces at work, are simply opportunities for us to become aware of our vulnerabilities so that we can grow into healthier relationships, mostly within ourselves. Sometimes they are to teach us to stand up for ourselves, or to step into our power. If we were to look back at those relationships from a completely honest perspective, we would find that we railed and kicked and screamed to stay in the relationship, even though it offered every opportunity to choose differently and very little of what we thought we needed at the time. We stayed because of some deceptive subconscious sense of need. We stayed because we feared the unknown possibilities of doing something different. We stayed in our comfortable discomfort.

We do resist change.

We often opt to stay in comfortable discomfort because the unknown scares us. But then being with someone who does not honor us, who uses or, worse, abuses us, is not okay. Really. Not okay.

The thing to do is recognize just why that experience has been perfect for our growth or expansion. When we look at the situation honestly and we don't like what we see, we might also ask ourselves why we are still there.

We have to leave the other person out of it for a minute. We can only be responsible for our own thoughts, feelings, and actions. No one makes us have them. What the heck are we doing? What untruths are we accepting in our own reckoning that cause us to stay in relationships that are so not good for us or the other person? Once we realize the answers to these questions, our path becomes clear, if we let it. And the relief of being free from the discomfort can be profound, and the self-discovery is priceless.

Sometimes partners just grow in different directions. Conversely, often one partner embraces life and grows tremendously while the other maintains the status quo, not seeming to need or seek change or expansion. Changes in the relationship begin to occur subtly, until one day the two people seem to have nothing in common at all. There is nothing wrong with this happening, it is simply two souls walking their life paths at their own paces with their own motivations and needs.

The important thing to remember is that if a relationship has run its course, and you honestly feel that working together (if both parties are willing to do so) won't change what is needed, it is okay to move on in life and sever the relationship.

Social morals and mores in the past have dictated that once two people are together, they are always together. These types of social and personal expectations cause great amounts of frustration and disharmony in couples whose relationship has truly run its course. It has also caused a lot of people to just settle, never having what they really wanted in life as they struggle to meet the expectations of society, their religion, or other social influences. Sometimes these social pressures cause couples to settle for each other, leaving in each of them a great chasm of emptiness of what they never experienced.

It is better to admit that the relationship is over than to torture each other indefinitely. There is nothing wrong at all about ending a relationship that has finished. Ending a relationship doesn't mean failure. Nor does it have to be a negative experience. Finishing relationships is simply part of life. If happiness is no longer available in the relationship, staying in a relationship is destructive to both people over the long term. No one has to be angry or mad. Relationships can end from the heart, responsibly and without threat to either party. After all, there was a lot of good in the relationship, right? You got together for some reason, right? Why dishonor that?

The question is, did you learn anything? Are you being honest with yourself about what the relationship brought, or are you continuing to deny, deny, deny?

To have relationships that are in truth and that have any chance of being fulfilling and of great depth, we must have a great relationship with ourselves first. We must love ourselves from our toenails up and to the depths of our very souls. We have to value ourselves beyond measure. We must be willing to see the truth of every situation in which we find ourselves, and we must be willing to stand in that truth, telling it with love both to ourselves and to our partners. We must never, ever believe that anyone has more power than we do, and we must be willing to expose our inner selves, our most vulnerable selves, to the essence of love. Otherwise, all of our relationships will be on the surface. We will always be defensive and feel that we are lacking.

Remember, no one can love you like you can, but they can come close if you give them a chance! When you are ready to expose yourself fully, first to yourself and then to another, you will attract someone who shares exactly what you are looking to find!

When having a relationship, remember, no one can fill you. If you look to someone to give you what you think is missing inside, you will be sorely disappointed. *But* if you enter into a relationship from a sense of fullness, you and your partner won't be able to help enhancing each other!

Exercise:
What Kind of Relationship Do I Want?

Take yourself to a quiet, comfortable place to sit. At your leisure, examine the following questions honestly with yourself. Even if you are already in a relationship, you may discover inner perceptions that are enhancing or interfering with your relationship.

What am I looking for in my lover (spouse, significant other, partner)? What kind of traits am I looking for in someone else? Do I have those traits? Do I use them?

What do I feel is missing in me that a/my partner can give? Why do I really feel like it is missing? Can I remember when I first felt that way? What happened then? Is how I feel now really because I feel like something is missing, or is it because I developed a perception the first time I felt like this? How can I feel full and whole without looking to someone else to fill my perceived gaps?

Do I really need someone in my life? If so, why? If not, why not?

What do I have to give to a relationship? What about me would attract another person?

Am I really willing to receive the love I want? Do I know how? If I feel funny about receiving, how will I ever have the full relationship I want? Am I willing to be open to my value?

Am I willing to communicate openly with my partner and share an equal relationship?

Chapter 11

Carry Your Own Baggage
(It's Too Heavy For Me!)

Certain dynamics, such as intimacy,
good communication techniques, honesty,
honor, and good intentions, are healthy and desirable.
But other dynamics can ruin or destroy relationships,
and even us, in the process.

How involved do we get in the pain of others because we feel sorry for them or are under the illusion that we can fix what is broken?

Many times relationships have a hero and a victim. The victim carries their past negative experiences like a badge of merit and an excuse for every poor behavior that they exhibit. The hero takes the position of caretaker to gain a perception of value. The hero creates a prison by being the responsible party, while the victim suffers in the prison by choosing to be there.

Soon, the pair falls into a very dysfunctional pattern: the hero enables the victim, and the victim enables the hero. And no one really wins.

The problem is that this dynamic stunts the potential development of either partner. A codependency is created, and both partners lose sight of self. The partner who perceives himself as damaged doesn't move past the bonds of pain and dependency. Clearly, the pain is exacerbated by the need to be taken care of. Seeing oneself as needy validates the perception of being incapable or not enough. The victim's sense of self-worth is fairly nonexistent, and their self-image is not pretty. Since their needs are being met by someone else, they don't need to make a real effort see themselves as well, whole, and strong; it becomes less important to have the things that they want. So the victim will remain in a state of perceived weakness or victimhood.

The hero, on the other hand, gains a false sense of power by being in charge, as well as responsible, and their sense of dominance is unquestioned by their weak partner. Knowing only how to give, the hero hasn't learned to receive and generally blocks their needs in order to gain a sense of importance. The hero doesn't usually know how to fully share on an emotional level because they are unable to reveal themself enough to really fully and deeply connect with their partner. Instead, they live on the surface, always being the "good guy."

In this kind of situation, balance is nearly impossible to maintain, and there is little to no growth by either partner.

Communication

Relationships are like Jell-O: When the environment is cool, they are resilient and bounce back to their original shape. But when the environment is too hot, relationships can quickly dissolve into an unrecognizable, sticky mess.

Our environment gets hot when we don't communicate our inner feelings, needs, wants, desires, likes and dislikes, or fears. When we keep everything in, no one has a clue who we really are or what we feel. Good communication is paramount to a healthy, balanced relationship. Too often we keep our mouths shut, not telling anyone anything deep or too important about ourselves, because it feels unsafe. We become vulnerable when we expose ourselves, making ourselves subject to having information used against us, which would inflict more pain than we already had. The fact is, in that moment we have given someone else more value than we give ourselves. By not speaking up, we tacitly say that someone else's wishes or needs are far more important than ours. *This is a lie!*

When we give our power to others, at some point, natural selection will force balance. But by then we will have lost our confidence and our joie de vivre and withered into unhappiness, or we will have settled for our lot in life.

> Living an unhappy, unfulfilled life is not what we came to Earth to do! We have come here to embrace our lives and live them fully and joyously!

If we have truly reckoned with ourselves and become honest inside ourselves, feelings of lacking safety dissipate, and we are left with solid ground to stand on.

Remember, learning to tell the truth can be difficult at first, but becomes easier the more we do it. It is as simple as telling one truth at a time, gaining confidence each time, and then telling the truth more until that is all there is.

As mentioned in chapter one, the main thing to remember is:

> The message is always dependent upon its delivery.

How we say what we mean has everything to do with how we are heard. If we speak from a perspective of defense, we will meet opposition from others. If we speak with love and acceptance, then we will receive loving acceptance back. (If we don't, we might want to consider who we are with and why.) If we speak with integrity, we have said our truth and offered it to be heard. If it is heard, then so it is. If not, then so it is. How others react to our truth says a lot about our relationships with them.

If what we have to say is considered and responded to in like fashion, then we know we have a caring, honest relationship. If our feelings, wants, needs, opinions, or anything else are being battled, then we know we are not being heard and, because of that, we are also not being honored.

Of course, we must communicate thoughtfully and without an agenda. We must make sure that our communications express our internal views and that we are not projecting our feelings and fears onto the other person. Sometimes when we haven't taken the time to develop an awareness of knowing what we really feel, we try to make others responsible for our baggage. This is also not acceptable, and yet it is extremely common.

> We must be self-aware enough that
> we can talk about our internal stuff without
> any attempt to make another person responsible
> for what is our doing alone.

We really have to own our stuff. Once we have done so, we become able to communicate with clarity.

In tandem with clear, honest communication come good listening skills. If we are so busy formulating our next defense or opinion, barely able to keep it in until it is our turn to speak, we aren't hearing the response we requested in the first place.

When we are uncomfortable in a situation, one of the first responses our body has is to briefly stop breathing. When we do hold our breath, our energy temporarily stops flowing, and the inside of our bodies becomes tense. Our emotions create a biological cycle, and as we continue to emote, chemical and electrical responses cause the cycle to intensify. This cycle of biological and emotional events strongly affects our response to the stimuli. So instead, breathe, relax, and listen to what is being said in response to your words.

Another part of solid communication is eye contact. When we speak to another, or interact in any way, we must look at that person directly. Looking into another's eyes says that we are present, interested, intentional, and on equal ground with the other person. The eyes also speak to the other on levels where there are no words.

When we connect eye to eye, we can recognize
the divine nature of each other and ourselves.

And when the divine is recognized, communication is definite.

Of course, we need to say what we mean. It is easy to look at the floor, or, more subtly, position our bodies in opposition to our words. Everything must match. And, of course, our actions must match our words. If we say something, then we must do or be that, whatever the case may be. One clear sign people aren't being honest is that their words and actions don't match. They might say one thing, but then exhibit another via their behaviors. This mismatch is a sure indication they are saying only the words they think you want to hear. Ultimately, they will go on to do what they want anyway, exhibiting no real change.

Our words, our actions, our thoughts, our heart of hearts—all must be in alliance with the sentiments we are sharing.

The Dynamics: Unresolved Issues

The dynamics of relations between human beings are intricate. When two or more lives blend, their stories can become entangled, streamlined, competitive, or synergistic as the details of the stories begin to unfold. Certain dynamics, such as intimacy, good communication techniques, honesty, honor, and good intentions, are healthy and desirable. But other dynamics can ruin or destroy relationships.

Control Issues

Control issues are one of the foremost dynamics in relationships. One or both parties have an inner need to know what is coming next and to make sure that everything happens according to those expectations. Because of this need, each party utilizes certain tactics in order to maintain a sense of control. A few of the more common modalities used for control follow.

Withholding Affection

Affection is withheld as punishment until the controlling person gets his or her way. This withholding is cruel and unnecessary. Affection between people, whether theirs is a friendship or a bonded love relationship, is vital to the balance and satisfaction of the relationship. Intimacy is a great part of the closeness people feel together. When one withholds affection, it belies selfishness and lack of trust. Further, withholding is a statement of higher value, meaning that the controlling partner is making a stand for dominance. This is not okay.

Subtleties

Subtleties are inferences or indirect remarks or behaviors that imply an outcome and are used to create doubt. Subtleties usually are directly related to manipulation. Manipulation of others often involves demeaning them for being who they are. This is not healthy. Manipulation is about not being honest enough with the self, and thus finding gentle authentic power, and instead gaining false power by belittling another by indirect nuances, manipulation, or outright direct comments. This is not acceptable in any relationship.

Direct communication is necessary for clear understanding and for the confidence of both parties. The more one is undermined, the more that person is likely to begin to keep secrets and lose a sense of self, placing power in the hands of the other. This is destructive and ultimately causes the controlling party to lose respect for the other.

Criticism

Criticism is used to undermine the confidence of another, generally because the critical person is insecure or has low self-esteem. Criticism gives the critic a false sense of power. It is unfair and unnecessary because both parties are entitled to be who they are in spite of their differences.

Rage

Rage is used to intimidate others and to gain a perception of power. Rage from an adult can be terrifying, and usually we avoid rage-filled confrontations at all costs. When rage is used against someone, it is not usually even about what is going on in the moment, but a deeper unacknowledged set of issues from the past. People who rage do not usually face their own issues, and gain a false sense of power by bullying others with their explosions. Trying to reason with someone who is enraged is generally impossible if the current experience is being addressed. Instead, it is best to understand the background and cause of the insecurity that triggers the rage in the first place. Fighting back with an enraged person can be dangerous and will not stop it; in fact, it will often incite them even further.

Jealousy

One of the most manipulative forms of control, jealousy is used to control what the partner does, with whom, when, and for how long. The jealousy is generally unfounded, and is used to keep a partner close at hand. Jealousy comes from fear of loss, abandonment, or rejection. It is completely fear based and can at times be irrational.

The truth is that the jealous partner could in fact have his or her own thoughts of straying to another but is projecting those thoughts onto the innocent partner.

A good sense of trust cannot be developed when jealousy rules the roost. Jealousy is destructive and can have opposite results. An untrusted partner, seeking fulfillment or even relief from the accusations of the jealous partner, might become involved with someone else after all. Ultimately, jealousy can cause the original imaginary scenario to become a reality.

Overall, control issues are highly destructive and create huge dysfunction in a relationship.

Other Destructive Dynamics

Adult-Child Behavior

In our psyche there is a child who, for whatever reasons, feels as if it is injured, somehow lacking in basic attention and needs—or perhaps is even spoiled. When it doesn't get what it wants, this child often acts out in our adult relationships. Coming through an adult body, this child can be daunting, terrifying, or simply a royal pain.

When we act from our child self, we are not taking responsibility for our actions. We expect someone else to fix what we think is wrong or give us what we need. We throw intimidating fits or perhaps even pick fights. Some adult children break things or act abusively toward their partners. *This is completely and equivocally not acceptable.*

The dysfunctional adult child operates from a dark place of need, or from a place of having been catered to as a child, and doesn't quite understand adult dynamics. To the adult child, everything that happens is someone else's fault. They find it impossible to own their own stuff. The best way to deal with this behavior is to be a loving mirror. A mirror—not a parent.

It is easy to fall into a parent role in response to this kind of behavior. Of course, acting like a parent is the worst thing we could do because it encourages the adult child to act out even more. Arguing gets you nowhere because, at least sub-consciously, the adult child has figured out every answer to every objection long before pitching that fit. Instead, it is best simply not to play that game. The child within the adult must learn that being an adult doesn't involve acting out or creating scenes.

The important thing is to get to the root of the issue if pos-sible. What is it about the situation that brought that child for-ward in the first place? Was the other person simply not getting his or her way, or is the situation actually related to something that happened in childhood? Is this a habitual behavior? What current need isn't being met, at least in that person's percep-tion? What is the child-adult afraid of, and how can that fear be allayed? How can that person provide for himself or herself without all the fuss?

Was some of this behavior the result of child abuse or sex-ual abuse? If so, then, first of all, the abuse can't be used as an excuse. Rather, the victim must work through the emotions of the abuse in a healthy and responsible way and, if neces-sary, with professional help. One does not need to relive past abuse or the pain of it to move past the abuse. Doing so simply requires finding a current sense of safety, which isn't always easy, but is possible!

Whatever the case, the inner child must learn skills that will enable it to learn to behave acceptably. When the child in your partner comes out, instead of reacting and fighting back , it is best to just not participate at all until the adult shows up again and is willing to talk responsibly.

Narcissism

Narcissism is another very frustrating behavior. Narcissists lives their lives almost entirely on the inside, keeping everything in, rarely and barely exposing their thoughts and feelings to others. Their whole world is about them. This behavior makes it impossible to reason with them, because when you do get communication, it is generally only their bottom line. Or they start in the middle of their reasoning process, and you never have any idea about how they got to that point, what affected them, or what triggered them or, worse, how to communicate with them.

By the time you experience their perceptions or behavior, it may seem very disconnected to what is currently happening, seeming to make little or no sense in the current situation. The narcissist's entire world is internal, and getting a glimpse is often painful. After all, they have internalized because they either don't have the life skills to make themselves feel safe when they are exposed, or they have so much pain from previous circumstances that they became bogged down, not knowing how to process that pain and never dealing with it at all.

To work better with someone who is narcissistic, open communication is encouraged. Ask pointed questions that are not attached to your hurt emotions. Get the other person to explain more thoroughly what he or she means and why. Explaining can be difficult for narcissists, so your patience will definitely be a virtue.

Narcissistic behavior isn't about you at all. It is about the narcissist's inability to bring forward what is within.

On the flip side, narcissistic behavior can also be a manipulative tool. On some level narcissists feel as if the less you know, the better. They feel more powerful within their secrets. Withholding information keeps their partners off balance enough that they become insecure and desperate for attention—and focus even more on the narcissist.

Projection

Projecting our feelings onto another person can cause us a lot of grief. Sometimes, without realizing it, we may actually accuse another person of exactly what we are thinking or feeling. Projection is generally a result of our not being honest with ourselves in the first place.

The truth is that when we start projecting our feelings onto others, we are afraid of or overwhelmed by whatever emotions we haven't yet recognized. If we can step back and take a look at what we are doing with an honest eye, we can realize that we are causing much of the situation ourselves.

Triangles

Triangles are dangerous games to play. Inadvertently, or even habitually, we sometimes add a third person into a relationship we share with someone else. This may be only from the stance of a friend's opinion, or could be an emotional affair. Often when there is a triangle, it is because we have difficulty committing ourselves to one situation with any depth. Or we need or are looking for something that our partner doesn't bring to the relationship but that another person provides very well.

Sometimes we add a third person to distract ourselves, or to dilute or defray the intensity of the relationship, and by doing so we often contribute to the other two participants' feelings of mistrust, jealousy, or downright hurt. Why? Because we are generally being dishonest, if even indirectly, first with ourselves and second with everyone else involved.

Further, each person in the triangle needs attention of some kind, and usually one person is trying to balance both of the other two. What results is jealousy, deceit, secrets, and imbalance all the way around. While triangles can have many facets and come up in most any type of relationships, they are all unhealthy and destructive. If you are in a triangle that is uncomfortable, make a choice. If you are worried about getting hurt or hurting someone, know that that is very likely to happen anyway. Separate yourself from the triangle or own your part in it, and be honest with both other parties. If each party is truly that connected with you, and your relationship with each is solid, everything will work out just fine. If not, then the relationships weren't founded in truth anyway.

This pattern is likely to be repeated more than once in your life. You can have what you need without closing yourself into this type of dynamic. You are too valuable to make yourself a pawn in a game of imbalance.

Compromising Yourself

Compromising yourself in a relationship can be deadly to both the relationship and your self-esteem. Compromising yourself is not the same as give-and-take on a specific issue with someone. Rather, it is giving up your values, dreams, wants, needs, desires, and anything else you can think of, in deference to another person. Giving up yourself leaves you powerless, out of control—and ultimately looking up one day and wondering where your hopes and dreams went and how to find yourself again.

Maintaining a sense of self is vital to sustaining yourself spiritually, physically, and mentally. No one has the right to expect you to be anything but who you are—no matter what.

If someone expects you to be anything but who you are, look at the relationship closely. Is it one you really want to be in?

Often when we stay in relationships that are not in our best interest we do so because we are addicted to the particular dynamics going on. Think about it. Think about relationships from your past. When you think of each person, what do you miss? Usually it is the things that made you crazy in the first place.

We often hold onto relationships out of a sense of desperation, feeling the unknown is worse than our comfortable discomfort. Sometimes it is best to just bite the bullet and leap into the chasm of the unknown. Take time for yourself. When your heart has had some time to heal, enter into the kind of relationship you want with someone who truly fits.

If you find yourself doing nothing but complaining about your relationship to others with nothing ever really changing, chances are you are living an addiction. The negative aspects of the relationship become tools for getting attention at the expense of your relationship and your partner.

If this is the case for you, try to identify what it is you need. What positive steps can you take to fulfill those needs in a more healthy way? Let go of the negative, even if it means being alone for a while. Get yourself together. Take time to get to know yourself. Your partner can never give you whatever it is that is causing you to seek attention in this way.

Exercise:
Turning Things Around

Think of one thing in your current relationship that really bothers you. If you are not in a current relationship, think of one thing in a previous relationship that troubled you. Behaviors, habits, ways of saying things, parts of the body, the way he ate, how she dressed, whatever—these can all be things that really get on our nerves.

Take a closer look at one thing (even if there are many to choose from), and ask yourself why it bothers you so much. Is it that you feel your partner's behavior reflects directly on you? Do you react because, as a child, you were punished for doing that same thing? For instance, when I was small, if I left a drawer or cabinet open or a chair pulled away from the dining table, I was corrected for doing so and even sometimes spanked. To this day I am hyper-vigilant about keeping cabinets and drawers closed and pushing my chair up to the table. This is definitely my stuff, but when my husband leaves the cabinets open, as he often does, I sometimes react internally and initially with a flash of anger. And then I realize: oh, I don't have to worry about that anymore. It is really okay if he leaves the cabinets open!

The point is to become aware of why you judge another's behaviors in the way you do. Then, if the behavior is truly rude, inconsiderate, or even unacceptable, you can address it accordingly with your partner.

Chapter 12

Dump Your Parent Issues
(No One Is Keeping Score!)

*If we really look at our behavioral patterns,
we can begin to see our parents in them.
What we need to remember is that, while many
of the values our parents taught us were good ones,
each of us is a soul who came to earth to have the
experience of life. Ours, to be lived as we choose.*

Once the wedding rings are in place and the reception is over, it is almost as if someone flips a switch and we become our parents. We react to our spouses the way our parents reacted to each other. We make decisions based on what our parents might have done. Often we even take on aspects of our parents' personalities. And most or all of this we do on a subconscious level.

All through our childhoods, we are glaringly and subtly conditioned to learn behaviors that our parents believed were right or that they inherited from their parents. This is not to say that no parents really had it together. Some did. On the other hand, most of our adult issues come from childhood, during which we were molded to fit the expectations of others often at the expense of our true natures.

Our parents' examples to us become us, and we embody the presence of our parents even when they are no longer there.

If we really look at our behavioral patterns, we can begin to see our parents in them. What we need to remember is that, while many of the values they taught us were good ones, we nonetheless have lives of our own and truths that are ours.

> We cannot live our lives fully when we are trying to be anything that we think someone else expects.

We are individuals with passions and choices all our own. We are souls who have come to this planet to have the experience of life. To do so, we must learn to live on our own terms— so we know what we want, what we need, and can go about our life experiences starting from a healthy and happy state of being.

Mimicking our parents robs us of experiencing our life journeys on our own terms. In fact, when we do follow the path of our parents, we quickly lose our sense of self, becoming unhappy and feeling unfulfilled often without knowing why. We begin to strive for something that is truly unobtainable, looking for approval in all the wrong places. We don't need approval; what we need is self-recognition.

Parent issues are some of the worst and most longstanding issues we can have. If we didn't feel nurtured as a child (and therefore still don't as an adult), we might look for a mother figure. If we never got enough, if any, of our father's attention, we might look for men whom we can look up to and who can give us what we think we need: approval, validation, value, or worse, someone to shoulder responsibility for us so we don't have to.

The truth is, once again, that no one can give us those things but us.

Parent dynamics in a relationship are more common than you might think. They are some of the most difficult to surpass because they are so ingrained in our subconscious. When children do not have what they need, they spend the rest of their lives trying to change that. After they become adults, their attempts to find those missing pieces can create sets of behaviors and dynamics between people that are frustrating and even painful. The most important advice is not to play into the parent role, which can easily sneak up on you.

For instance, a man marries a woman who is very strong, decisive, and powerful. He does not feel he has these traits because he lacks a strong mother figure. Everything is hunky-dory until the honeymoon is over. Then, when the new wife acts from within her innate power, the very thing he was attracted to in the first place, he throws a fit and does something unacceptable to retaliate. She immediately reprimands him, and before you know it, mother and son are acting together all over again.

Conversely, say a woman didn't get the acknowledgment she felt she needed from her father. Perhaps he worked two jobs or was emotionally inept. Perhaps he left the family when she was a child. Whatever the case, she marries a man just like him and pretty soon feels her marriage is lacking. She does things for her husband's approval and sometimes even makes a list of her daily accomplishments in order to be recognized, but she still goes unnoticed and wonders why. She becomes a royal nag, he is pushed further and further away, and the marriage frazzles. Her biggest fear of being unnoticed and unimportant has become reality . . . again.

A lot of dynamics can fall into the parent-issue department. A hypochondriac, someone who is always sick, is looking for attention and usually gets it until their counterparts get tired of the game or, worse, enable the behavior. Someone who is an eternal victim also craves attention and doesn't have the skill to get it in positive form. The same goes for those people who make themselves omnipotent, loud, and always right, while on the inside they are terrified of being wrong.

Whatever the issues or origins, all of them can be overcome with self-honesty and an honest effort to dissociate from habitual patterns. If you recognize any of these patterns in yourself, look to the root cause and deal with the accompanying fears. Once identified, the vulnerabilities and their protracted issues can be alleviated.

The greatest awareness of all is being able to recognize these issues in us or in others—and not playing them. Becoming aware of and willing to change our habitual and dysfunctional behaviors, and understanding and choosing to relate differently with those of our partners, can be the beginning of an entirely new and different type of relationship.

The Bottom Line for Healthy Relationships

If we haven't dealt with our inner issues, we will carry them into every relationship we have.

We must view our friends, lovers, partners, and others with a sense of equality, honoring and respecting them as we expect them to do for us. We must see ourselves in an equal light to our partners, no matter what.

We have to leave room in any relationship for both parties to maintain their personal interests and sense of individuality. We need time to explore our curiosities, to revitalize our senses of excitement. Ultimately, when both partners are free to be who they are, the interest in a relationship is ongoing. There is more to talk about, and the relationship can expand in its depth at a natural rate. Our sense of self is vital to our functioning and healthfulness. When we lose that, we have no resources from which to work.

We must be willing not only to communicate honestly, but also to listen well. Open and honest communications will alleviate most fears. Honesty in any relationship is paramount to its success. Once a sense of mistrust develops, the relationship is doomed. Honest is the only way to be.

Fairness and openness to new ideas and circumstances are very important. Being fair and willing to give-and-take, as long as balance is maintained, is excellent.

A great relationship has passion, not just in the bedroom, but also in life. Excitement for each other often becomes lost in the course of everyday living. Work schedules can get in the way as well. My suggestion is make regular dates with each other and do new and different things. Don't always go to the same places; that gets boring. Plan getaways regularly, if possible, or even try weekends with a theme.

Be willing to gracefully accept for yourself as much as you give. If you don't, you are robbing your partner of the joy of giving to you. Know you have value that is infinite!

Have no expectations, as they will only set you up for disappointment. Stay in the now, not what was or might be. Be willing to be flexible with your partner. Schedules change, as do interests and focus. Be willing to go with the flow no matter what.

Do not judge your partner in comparison to yourself. You are two different people who came together to complement each other. Judgment begets inequality, and inequality is disastrous to any relationship. Honor your friends, lovers, family, and children as the priceless treasures they are!

Be *now*. Stay present in all your relationships. Don't go looking for problems . . . and for heaven's sake, don't ask everyone else about your relationship. Keep it between you and your partner. Remember that everyone has an opinion and an agenda that are not necessarily in your favor or in the interest of the health of your relationships. Many relationships are torn apart once others start injecting their two cents. Trust your partner. Be sensitive to what is happening inside you and what those in your relationships are experiencing. Be connected.

Be happy! Don't always look for what you don't have. Be now and find the positive in everything around you. Everything that you need is on the inside. No one else can give you what you don't give yourself. Be now. Do what you want. Be a partner, not the enemy. Live your relationship to its fullest potential.

Relationships don't just happen. They blossom with the participation of those involved. Sometimes that takes some work, but the results can be far worth it. Be strong when necessary and soft every moment that you can. Stay in your heart, especially when your fears rear up to bite you. Remember that your partner wasn't likely there when those fears were born. Don't make your partner responsible for them!

Love deeply your friends, spouses, lovers, partners, your children. Love with all that you are, but first of all, love yourself just as you are. You are an amazing, perfect, whole human being just as you are!

Exercise:
Examining My Motivations
for Relationship

Ask yourself what it is that you seek in others. What traits do you look for in your friends and love relationships? Write them down, perhaps in a list. Once you have identified the traits in others, ask yourself if you acknowledge the very same ones in yourself. Write this down as well. Look at your answers carefully! If you don't recognize these traits within you, look at why. What is it that you feel you need from other people that you don't already have? As you discover each of the traits you feel you lack, look at various ways to apply them to your life experience from your own internal resources. Find ways to use these traits in your life.

Chapter 13

Have It All
(What Are You Waiting For?)

Everything that came before us
is encoded within every cell of our bodies.
In addition, the infinite possibilities
of our future are also
resident within us.
All we need to do is choose our direction,
then step willingly into our journeys.
Sometimes we must
step forward out of pure faith,
not having a clue where we are going.
We know what to do.
We always have.

We dream. We imagine. We want, desire, wish—and sometimes those things become reality, but not usually. Sometimes it seems like . . . we . . . almost . . . get . . . there and then boom! Something, or a series of somethings, stops us in our tracks. Why is that?

How can we have anything we want? Only lucky people get everything they want, right? No!

The purest process of creation is right here all of the time. The possibilities are infinite. Can we accept what we want? Do we deserve what we dream? What if someone else doesn't do his or her part? What if? Why not? Why is it that the things that we want don't happen?

Creation Is a Harmonic Field

If we are going to successfully create the kind of life we want and live our dreams and desires, we must first recognize the power we have in the creative process. The success of the film and the book *The Secret* is an indication that millions of people are ready for change in their lives. When we are ready for change it is because we are bored, not getting what we want, or craving more challenge. The Secret is telling the truth. What the authors did not explain is how and why the Secret works. Here is the secret to the Secret: There is no secret.

Each of us is made up of a set of harmonic frequencies of light, color, and sound. This composition is a lot like an intricate musical chord. Every one of us is a unique chord in all of creation. No two people are harmonized quite the same. That is why we are attracted to some people right away and repelled by others immediately.

The rest of creation, all matter, is a lot like a page of blank sheet music, on which we draw the chords that create a musical composition—in this case, our lives. The page is the glue that holds the symphony of us together. The lines where we put the notes are directions of communication with definite messages. And while we read the music from left to right, creation senses from every direction at once, seeking information about what to do next along infinite pathways. Because of this, each of us is an intricate and necessary part of all creation.

In turn, creation is communicating with us on elaborate levels everything that we need to know. Creation adds to our symphony, bringing to us intricacies that gel to become reality.

Each of us is extremely important;
without every one of us as part of the composition,
the symphony can't exist.

Written on a page of musical composition are not only the notes and the chords, but also all the instructions about how to play each part. Which instruments to be played and when, the mood, the pace, whether the music should be expressed softly or with vigor, all of it.

When we create our own symphony, in this case, how we live our lives, we literally create a set of instructions detailing what we want our lives to be like, how they will feel, what instruments will make it whole, and how beautifully every note will come together as we express our feelings within each experience as life progresses. As we write our life symphony the rest of creation obliges by bringing to us exactly what we need for the grand performance.

The most wonderful part of our creative process is that we have everything available to us that we could possible need. The music of everything that came before us is within every cell of our bodies. In addition, the infinite possibilities of our future are also resident within us. In any given moment we can draw upon that plethora of information to change what happens next.

Everything that has ever happened anywhere, any time is written in the complexity of the harmonics of creation. All of that information is stored in different frequencies of light. Imagine—the entirety of endless history current to real time now, and infinite possibilities for the future, contained in an intangible library we can access any time we choose!

Because we are made of the same stuff as everything else, we have the memory of everything that has ever happened inside us. We literally have an invisible set of instructions inside that helps us choose our life experiences.

More importantly, that same instruction book tells us where to go next, how to get there, and even who we are in relation to everything else in creation. The information comes to us as intuitive guidance, thoughts from left field that have nothing to do with what else we happen to be thinking in the moment.

We can literally draw upon the infinite to clarify what we need, want, or desire simply because it is us and we are it. We are infinite beings of a greater whole intertwined as part of an unbounded weaving that is part of an infinite choreography that is more complex than our thinking minds can grasp. Creation is listening to us 24/7. The question is, are we listening?

For the purpose of even greater understanding, imagine that creation is a repetitive pattern of predictable geometric shapes on both the smallest and the grandest levels of existence. The basic fabric of creation is based upon the shape of an octahedron, which looks like a ball with eight flat sides. The octahedron is composed of eight four-sided pyramids. The pyramids have a system of light and harmonics just like we do. Each individual structure, first the pyramid and then the octahedron, has an individual set of harmonics that is a separate consciousness from all other particles.

As the octahedronal particles come together to change reality into matter, they harmonize according to the instructions they have received. The octahedrons organize with a flat side to flat side alignment based upon positive and negative polarities, like at each end of a battery or a magnet. As the octahedrons align, a new and different reality is formed. That reality is expressed in creation as a conveyance of energy that takes shape as mass. Or, as an analogy, an idea (a thought) is an expression, and the outcome of that idea is reality. As a whole structure, reality looks a lot like this:

The Fabric of Creation:
Our Map to Creative Imagining!

As you might notice from the figure above, between the octahedrons are empty spaces. We'll call these the null zones. It is in these spaces that our thoughts, prayers, and intentions travel. As we make an expression of desire of any kind, that expression travels as energy through the null zones. As it does, the octahedrons, which are also energy, receive the messages. As the messages are received, the octahedrons begin to wobble in place and rearrange to re-harmonize and create a different reality.

We Talk to Creation and It Talks Back!

How we communicate our wants and desires into the creative process has everything to do with the outcome. Most of the time when we mean to create a new experience or event in our lives, we do so with concerns, worries, and even fear. We place the responsibility of each outcome as dependent upon other things, such as others doing their part. Basically, we create with an entire set of what-ifs.

Without necessarily meaning to, we often precondition our wishes using subconscious input such as our fears. Maybe we don't truly feel we deserve what we want. Maybe we feel that someone else has to participate for our wishes to come true. Maybe we . . . ? The ways we can sabotage our creative process are unlimited.

We also repeat our requests over and over again, wishing, hoping, wanting, even needing. And yet, things don't quite work out. Part of the reason this is true is because we focus on the process and not the outcome.

If we focus on the process, what we communicate to creation is that we don't believe in the outcome we stated, and therefore the outcome as a pending reality becomes weakened, then nebulous, and finally falls apart, never happening at all.

Affirmations are statements we say over and over again so we can continue to believe in and be reminded of a specific outcome. Do you use affirmations to create life events of what you want? Yes? Well, never *ever* use them again.

Affirmations create dependence and are crippling. Affirmations are crutches that maintain our sense of need.

The reason that this is so is because each moment we exist, we are literally different from the way we were only a moment before. We are constantly re-harmonizing to our environments, other people, everything. When we make a statement in one moment we do so with a specific set of energetic harmonics. When we repeat ourselves later, we are harmonically different, so our request is communicated differently as well. Not only are we harmonically different, our thoughts and feelings are changing in every moment as well.

When we repeat ourselves with a different set of thoughts and feelings, we change the original message and confuse the creative process. Instead of the particulates changing position to create the reality we wanted, they wobble in place without rearranging, and we receive little to no benefit from our intentions. Or worse, we get chaos that looks like we might get what we want but it fizzles out and never fully happens. The chaos happens but we never really get to the outcome. Without realizing it, we have created a harmonic loop in which the same information processes over and over again without resolution. Little do we know that the fizzle was our own doing!

How we present our desires to the creative process is a big deal. If we are *asking*, that means it only *might* happen or we may succeed. Asking also means that something or someone outside of us is responsible for the change we want.

Nothing and no one outside of us
gives us our experiences.
Only we give our experiences to ourselves.

Asking suggests subservience. To ask denies our personal power of creation. Remember that we are whole and perfect beings of creation. Having the kinds of experiences we want is our birthright. We have free will and the ability to imagine infinite kinds of realities. We are the creator that we seek. Therefore we don't ask; we command.

That which we seek also seeks us.

Everything we desire is already available to us. By virtue of the fact that we aspire to it at all, our desire became a reality. But if we don't believe in our creative process then what we want will never be so. We must believe without a doubt, completely and fully in everything that we intend to create . . . and then let it go.

Right about now you are probably wondering "What does she mean, let it go?" That is exactly what I mean. Sending a prayer or intention into the universal process to create a reality is a lot like throwing a ball. Simplified, your intention is a living thing. It is real, it is alive, and it is of your desire. That intention is the impetus to your new reality. It is the fuel to the fire, the water to the drought. To allow your intention to grow, it needs to be fed, just like all other living things. The kind of nourishment it requires is passion.

We can literally hold our intention in our hand, fill it with the imagining of how we will feel when we have arrived in our new experience, fill our desire with the passion of the feeling of experiencing it, with no doubt or fear and then . . . let it go. Send that intention sailing into creation!

Passion of the heart is the fuel of all creation.

We have to pray *and* move our feet. How true that is! As we send our command outward into the infinite, we must believe and know, without a doubt, that it is already so. We must know we have created a reality, and now must do our part toward meeting that reality in a moment in time when our current path and the reality that we have created intersect. As that intersection occurs, we have our new reality exactly or better than we had imagined.

The real key here is not to have expectations. No expectations? No, none. When we have expectations, we set ourselves up for a pass/fail situation. We get exactly as we expected or less. Nothing more. If we do not set parameters of expectations, we allow any number of infinite possibilities to come together for a reality even greater than we could have imagined!

I will tell you a great story. Years ago when I left my hometown to be with my husband, I had given my car away to someone who needed it. I wasn't going to need one for a while. Several years after that I was very sick and not able to work for a long period of time. In the meantime, my husband was transferred to another state nearly three thousand miles away.

After we moved and I began to heal and become strong again, I began to feel trapped without a car. I had enough money in the bank for an old used car, but that was about it. I had just started working again and wasn't sure how much a month I could afford in the way of car payments.

I began to search in earnest on the Internet for cars for sale in my general vicinity. It was a tedious process to say the least. I was sitting at my computer screen, exasperated, when I heard, "Go to the Lexus dealer!" Oh, yeah, right, like I even have enough to talk with those people let alone buy a car from them (but a Lexus *was* what I had secretly wanted for years!).

I doubted my guidance, talking to myself. "Yeah right, like I really have the means to go buy a car at the Lexus dealer." And then another thought crossed my mind . . . "Well they probably do get great quality trade-ins . . . maybe they have something affordable . . . ?"

My husband had promised to take me out to find a vehicle on Saturday. My anticipated day came around and we got in the car to go to town. The conversation went something like this:

"So, where do you want to go?"

"Take me to the Lexus dealer, please"

"*What?*" Eyes twinkling (he knows me by now).

"Yes, please, take me to the Lexus dealer. I heard I could get a great deal there." I didn't tell him who told me.

We arrived at the dealer and met a great salesman. I was honest to the guy from the word go. "Look, I may not be your biggest sale of the day, but if you treat me right, within two years I will be back and that next sale will be well worth your while!" No response. He wasn't impressed. But he did show me three awesome possibilities.

That day it worked out that I got a practically new car with everything, and I mean *everything,* that I could have imagined if I had actually ordered the car I wanted. Only a year old, few miles, leather interior, all of the bells and whistles you can imagine and it even still smelled new.

It wasn't the Lexus but it was fantastic. Apparently there were so many auto dealers in the area that every Saturday they ran an ad for one or two cars priced under book value as an incentive to get potential buyers in the door. I was lucky enough to get there early and buy that incentive car! Not only that, but two years later I was back to upgrade to my new Lexus, because I believed it with all my heart and my intention became reality.

I had left my options open by not defining the outcome too specifically. Instead, the message I had sent was nothing more than the feeling I would have driving my new car.

When we send a clear message out to creation,
we get a clear response—a successful manifestation
of the reality we meant to create.

Faith has everything to do with our creative power. Faith is nothing more than a solid belief in something that we can't see or understand. If we want to be successful in our creative endeavors, we must believe fully and completely that what we have intended is done!

One of the words that comes up a lot when I work with clients is "abundance." According to Bing.com dictionary, "abundance" means: 1. Large amount, A more than plentiful quantity of something; 2. Affluence, A lifestyle with more than adequate material provisions; 3. Fullness, A fullness of Spirit that overflows.

And yet I hear this word most when it is spoken by people who don't value themselves. The concept of abundance has escaped them on every personal level. To them, abundance is something that comes from outside of them. They are self-perceived victims of a world that doesn't give them what they want.

They want, they need, and yet they don't value themselves to any degree. Beating themselves up for what they haven't done, gained, or accomplished, self-criticism is their norm. Many appear defeated. The truth is that abundance is value, period. Money is value. Even joy is value. We are value. How can we attract value when we don't value ourselves?

Get What You Give!

The first thing that has to happen if we are going to have what we want is that we have to know, without a doubt, that we deserve anything and everything we want. To do this means we must accept not only the possibility that we are perfection, but the reality that we are, beyond a shadow of a doubt, the most miraculous creature in all creation.

We must be willing to receive as easily as we give.

Most of us give to others quite easily. We give our time, our energy, even our belongings away, but when it comes to receiving, that can be difficult. If we have trouble receiving it is because we have not acknowledged our value.

Our sense of personal value is easily reflected in our ability to receive. When we say things like, "Awww, you shouldn't have," or "I don't deserve this," or "I can't believe you did this," we are literally reinforcing our belief that we are less than and not deserving. When we receive something from another person, it also doesn't mean that we owe them in return. There is a vast difference between a prearranged honest exchange and someone just doing something nice for you.

Gratitude

Learning to receive is nothing more than simply knowing we are worth whatever the circumstance and learning to be gracefully *grateful*.

When we have gratitude we open the door
to more and greater gifts in our lives.

Gratitude is a gift in itself. When we remember to be grateful we are saying that, yes, we are perfection and, yes, we deserve what we get and, yes, bring more at every opportunity! Gratitude comes in all forms for all reasons. We can be grateful for:

- What we have
- What we don't have
- What is now
- Things we have learned
- Things we still need to learn

- The love we give
- The love we receive
- Our lives
- Our successes
- Our challenges
- Our health
- Our families
- Our friends
- Our ability to imagine
- Our free will
- Our perfection

. . . the list is infinite.

Exercise:
Gratitude, Creating, and More Gratitude

First of all, take a deep breath. Think of ten things for which you are grateful. Let that gratitude expand your heart space. Terrific.

Next, think of something that you want or need. Imagine you have put that thing into your hand. Hold it gently. Imagine how you will feel when you are in the reality of your creation. Next, close your eyes and bring the feelings of gratitude into your hands with your creation. Now, throw it away from you. As your intention travels further and further away, know that as it is, it is getting closer and closer to returning to you as a full-blown reality. Relax, breathe, and know without a doubt that your intention is now a reality, that you and it will meet in time. Remember to watch for the signs in each moment as to how you can participate toward the coming moment of manifestation of your reality, and know that it is done.

How long does it take for your reality to occur? How completely do you believe in your creation? Sometimes it is instantaneous; at other times, it takes a little while. Only you can determine the outcome. How completely do you believe in your creation?

Chapter 14

Embrace Your Gifts
(Express Yourself!)

What we call our gifts are nothing more
than our inherent abilities coming to light.
They are our birthright.

The main reason we often begin to feel as if we don't fit in or don't belong is because of our inner gifts—our sensitivities, intuition, awareness, and abilities to express honestly and completely what is in our hearts and minds at any given moment.

Some of us have always had a great sense of being different, that we just don't fit in with the scope of humanity. We feel as if we need to be somewhere else or even to "go home." But where is that? Some of us began having otherworldly visions or intuitive knowledge as far back as we can remember. But then our parents and others told us those things weren't real, and we began to feel set aside, hiding our encounters. Sometimes we feel things so deeply that nothing in our language could express the profundity of our experience.

No matter what we have gone through or continue to go through, all of the incidents reflect the gifts we have inside of us. These gifts can become excellent tools for a greater life experience, or we can choose to become victims of them.

It is time to wake up to the fact that we are, each and all, filled with abilities and gifts that don't make much sense, yet we know and feel things that on some level of reality are very real.

Most of us have had some sort of out-of-the-ordinary experiences that made us wonder or, worse, that made us afraid because we didn't understand what was happening. We all have the innate ability to look, see, hear, and feel beyond what we understand and into the realms of the infinite. Just because we had experiences doesn't mean we are weird or set aside. Instead, our experiences confirm that, yes, we are part of a greater whole. And that is just fine.

Our Gifts Are Tools for Life

First of all, our gifts are simply abilities. Some of our abilities are remarkable, while others seem more mundane. There are a multitude of gifts we might have. There are the very human ones, like compassion, creativity, resilience, drive, tenacity, patience, practicality, responsibility; the ability to laugh, to see things as they really are, to move with ease through life's challenges, to have command of our bodies, minds, and spirits, to love, to live at all . . . just to name a few.

And there are other kinds of gifts too. The ones many people don't yet understand but which are as real as all those named above. These days more and more of us are realizing we have another set of senses that comes to us naturally. These are what I call our higher senses. These kinds of senses are related to our more intuitive nature. These gifts may include the ability to know things in advance, or to know what people really mean even when they don't say it. Others may include the ability to feel or experience the energy of people, places, and things, to see or even communicate with people who have passed on, or with beings in other dimensions. Some may see colors, or feel the pain of others. There are a myriad of ways these kinds of gifts might unfold for any given person.

Some of us have had these gifts available to us all our lives and they seem as natural to us as breathing. Others of us find we are opening to these different senses as if being reborn with a new and different way of seeing the world. Many call this happening awakening.

We have come to a time in human evolution when those parts of us that have been sleeping for millennia are rising to the surface as natural parts of our being. Unfortunately, the immediate reaction of many who begin to awaken is fear, and, second, to keep these experiences a secret, hiding them from most others. I have seen many people become victims of themselves, not realizing that these new and different senses are as normal as breathing and can be great contributions in combination with everyday life.

Used as a natural part of daily existence, our intuitive nature can contribute nuances to us we might not otherwise have been aware of. Conversely, we can become victims of our abilities. *So what* if your dead grandmother comes to you in your dreams? (Did she have a message for you? If so, did you listen?) *So what* if you knew something before it happened? (Did you follow your intuition and avoid disaster?) *Who cares* if you hear someone talking to you about things you don't know about? (What if the information is good and helps you?) *What if* your intuition was right, and what you thought you knew was, in fact, *really true*? (Is saying "I knew it!" enough, or is there something greater happening that maybe we haven't realized yet?)

If this is happening to you, stop holding your breath and thinking that all of a sudden you are more divine or talented than other human beings. You aren't. It is true that you are a magnificent creature of the One, as divine as you are human. The fact is that these kinds of experiences are part of our innate being. We are born with these abilities and had simply forgotten how to use them—or that we even had them.

We *all* have the ability to have these experiences. The question is, do we use these abilities as easily as we do our most commonly understood senses of seeing, hearing, smelling, touching, and tasting? The truth is that you are simply becoming who you have always been. More to the point, when you have experiences like the ones mentioned above, you are remembering *more* of who you are. These are gifts that are simply part of who you are.

Besides hiding their intuitive natures, a second kind of reaction occurs to those experiencing awakening. That is the belief that, if we can know things, feel energy, help heal others, we must go out, barefoot and poor, proselytizing and giving ourselves away in service to humanity until we drop. *Really?* Yes. This comes from religious teachings that have been ingrained in us that we are sinners, imperfect and second to God and all creation when, in fact, we are aspects of that, acting as only aspects of God and the living one could act . . . by being innately in tune with all other things. Don't get caught up in the dogma and ensuing emotional trauma that comes with it. These kinds of abilities are as normal as breathing. They are nothing more than awareness of or the ability to connect with others on an unseen level. Here is the deal:

We are created of all things, all things are created of us,
and therefore each of us is an integral part of all creation,
unique in our reflection of it.

That being said, why then would we see ourselves in our intuitive nature as anything but being who we are? Instead, we can learn to understand or at least become comfortable in our higher nature, to let it unfold in the way of experience and realizations and celebrate that we have found a piece of our light that is interactive and our right as children of creation. There was never meant to be a comparison of each other, what we can or can't do. People invented that to feel important or insignificant, to control each other.

Each of us is a unique and perfect being, the perfect reflection of the marriage of the human and the divine and reflected in reality with free will and the powers of observation and choice.

Our sensitivities can actually help guide us in our lives. A gut reaction to something is a gift. That reaction is telling us to pay attention. Danger! Danger! Or, Yes! Yes! We must look past the illusion and see what that reaction is telling us.

But do we listen? Our bodies tell us more than we realize. At the first sign of a situation that is out of bounds with our inner truth, our bodies tense, usually either in the chest or abdomen. We hold our breath for a moment. And then, well, we either listen to our bodies or ignore them and plunge right into a situation that ultimately isn't good for us.

Our internal gifts help us to see whether we are on the right track or straying into dangerous territory. Our intuition doesn't just happen once in a while. It is there all the time, prodding us to pay attention, but often we ignore its message as a crazy thought or a passing erroneous piece of information. Only later, of course, do we find out that we were right in the first place!

Our human habit of mentally processing everything is part of our survival mechanism and keeps our intuition at bay. Thinking sets up an entire set of nerve-firing patterns in our brains, and that pattern locks the doors to our higher knowing. When we defend ourselves by being "rational," thinking through things over and over again, the truth is lost, and we step into directions that aren't necessarily good for us.

Being present in the now really helps. By that I mean not looking outward in anticipation or concern about what will happen later, or looking into the past to try and understand what the heck happened. Have all of our attention right here, right now.

It isn't as easy as we think. *But* if we allow our innate gifts to come forward, we have all the discernment we need and all the awareness necessary to make great decisions or to just go with the flow.

Being in the now and letting our natural abilities guide us is pure freedom to the nth degree. We can relax into the now without worry or concern and begin to notice all the opportunities that come our way. We are released from our self-imposed chains and are able to live freely.

Living in the now is the ultimate definition of faith. When we are able to simply trust that we are perfect and doing the perfect thing in every moment, magic happens.

Magic is everywhere! The only question is, do we notice?

We Are Sacred Beings

When we begin to notice the magic, we begin to see the little clues in every now that direct us, connect us, guide us to the most exquisite choices that open our lives into fullness and completeness. We begin to operate from our sacred selves. After all, we are created of all that is holy.

Now I don't mean "holy" in a religious sense. Unfortunately, religion allows only for the elite—saints and prophets, priests, initiates, and other singularly identified people to carry a recognized designation of "holy." The truth is that "Holy" is a place each of us has inside that is an unlimited expression of love, that love being our connection with our source. We feel holy when we consciously connect with our divine nature. What I mean is that we are sacred beings who are created from all that is divine and therefore have the ability to feel that very thing within us while we exist as aspects of the same.

One very clear definition for the word *sacred* (taken from *dictionary.net*) is: "Designated or exalted by a divine sanction; possessing the highest title to obedience, honor, reverence, or veneration; entitled to extreme reverence; venerable."

We are that: sacred in every sense of the word. It is only our perspectives that warp our sense of the sacred in others and ourselves. Since we are created of the divine, we can consider ourselves innately sanctioned. And if we are divinely sanctioned, we can be nothing but sacred by virtue of our existence.

Even if we have not recognized our inner perfection, we remain constructed of particles of the infinite that have manifested as matter and become animated into the form of human being. There is no escaping our origin. We are living representations of the divine.

Since we are all holy, we all have the innate and indelible right to be who we are, with our free will and immense gifts, to create a life that is fully abundant and exuberant—then what are we waiting for? Let's drop the pretense that we are anything less than perfect and get on with living from a sense of sacred perfection.

Whatever glimpses we may have had beyond the reality that we describe as normal are simply reminders that there is much more than we currently remember. There is so much potential in what we *don't* know. All we must do to find this place within us is to relax into our experiences and remember that it is all perfection.

Exercise:
Returning to the Divine Perspective

Think of yourself as a divine being. What is your first reaction? Disbelief? Do you want to laugh? Do you feel that this can't be true because you are so imperfect?

Look again. Look deeper. Close your eyes. Breathe. Ask yourself to reveal the hidden you. Keep breathing. Let your breath rise into your heart, opening it slowly until you feel as if you will burst. You won't.

Send your attention into your full heart. Breathe in the feeling of fullness. How does that feel? Keep doing it. Allow yourself to float freely in your heart space for as long as you desire. In this state, you have returned to the divine. Breathe this feeling throughout your body until you feel intensely light in every cell. Accept that whoever you are, whatever you do, you are a whole and perfect child of creation and nothing or no one can ever change that but you. And even then, the only thing you can really change is your perception.

Chapter 15

The Art of Being a Magnificent Human Being

(You Know Who You Are, and That's All That Matters!)

You are a whole and perfect being of creation.
There is no limit to what you can be.
You need no one's permission but your own.

A journey through the heart and soul brings us revelations and realizations about behaviors and issues we didn't know we had. We begin to find freedom, first from our own binding perceptions and then from the perceptions of others, as we learn to eject our old tapes and learn new patterns of behavior. We begin to understand just how complex our defense systems have become.

The truth is that everything is simple.

Life. Every bit of it.

When we understand just how tightly bound we have become simply by doing or being the "right thing," we are likely astounded. We realize that we had lost our way and were on a nebulous path to Never Never Land via Mr. Toad's Wild Ride.

If you do nothing else, take the tools in this book and work with them. None of them is too hard, and all of them are beneficial for changing your life into anything and everything that you can imagine.

We have learned to accept ourselves just as we are, knowing that who and what we are is the truth and everything anyone has told us beyond that is an illusion created to maintain superiority. We are perfection regardless of what anyone else thinks.

We have looked at how telling the truth sets us free, and that while being truthful takes a little practice, when we are truthful we no longer have to cover our tracks or feel insignificant. Honest communication is paramount to healthy relationships, as is the ability to learn how to discern what the truth of them is. Our ability to know the truth is innate. Let the truth ring out loud and clear, with equal amounts of passion and compassion.

We have realized that our fears often run our entire lives, and we have learned how to identify those fears, owning them so we can finally let them go. Recognize your inner fears and make it okay to talk about them, so that you are less stressed and can become confident in yourself.

Our passion had eluded many of us, but we have realized that passion is a multitude of things, and underneath all of those possibilities is a heart open to whatever we experience. Be exuberant, even when you feel it is silly. Realize that self-expression is honest and not something to hide away.

We have learned that it is fine to question everything and that asking questions relieves the tension of holding in our fear of what we don't understand. Ask thoughtful, intentional questions and, in turn, listen to the answers. Have your own opinions and know that whether anyone else agrees or disagrees isn't important.

Together we have come to the realization that we can finally stop fixing ourselves, that all of the self-help in the world isn't going to help anything if we don't truly grasp its meaning and apply it to our life experiences. We have learned how to identify within ourselves that which we need to know for our own perspectives and to make more positive decisions. Know that no matter what anyone else says or does, their actions are based solely on opinions—theirs—and do not need to cause you injury or loss of confidence.

We have studied all of the reasons we don't need to fear change, and why the result of change is magnificence. We now know why we should let the flow carry us into the unknown, filled with excitement at the prospect of the infinite possibilities available to us when we just let ourselves go. We know that we don't have to resist, we only have to be in the now, for now is all there ever is. Create some kind of change every day. Step off the pinnacle into the unknown with excitement as you consider the infinite possibilities that are open to you because of those changes.

We have learned that we can have it all, and we can laugh the entire way through our life journeys. Remember to look up and into the eyes of others and to have a sense of humor about what you see. Remind yourself that you can create whatever you want in life and that whatever you can imagine is already so.

Perhaps we are now more aware of how we interact in all the relationships in our lives. Maybe, just maybe, we can begin to recognize the dynamics at play around us as others act out their stories. Relationships can be whole and healthy, and filled with joy. Leave behind the idea that anyone can fill any part of you; remember that your fullness comes from you.

We have become aware of how we create our inner stories to keep us from truths we don't want to see. We know now that those truths are far greater than the deceit causing us ongoing pain. Tell yourself the truth even when it hurts. You will be a far greater person for having learned the power of the truth, and with the recognition and comfort of that truth you will know others much more thoroughly as well.

Our gifts are part of who we are, and should be embraced, honored as part of the sacred in each of us. You are very, very special. Different is fabulous, no matter how it looks. Don't turn away or be frightened by what you don't understand. Stand up and celebrate yourself and everyone every day.

Our lives are ours to live, and what anyone else thinks, says, or does is subject to our discernment and approval. Remember this always, and honor *you* first, regardless of anything else. When you take time to honor yourself, so will everyone else.

Lighten up on yourself. Remember that there are no secrets. We can have whatever we want. And we want a lot for ourselves, so why not go for it? What we find will become the framework for the rest of our lives. When we get real, the art of living out loud is not only easy, but fun and infinitely rewarding!

Afterword
(But Not the Last Word)

Recently, during a trip to Scotland, I took a group on a journey of very sacred sites there. As we were standing in the midst of one of the stone circles, or henges, and I observed the individual experiences happening within the group members, I had a most profound revelation. After they had their private moments, the group encircled me, expecting to hear something wise and spiritual. What came out of my mouth was a surprise to everyone there, including me.

I would like to repeat it here, leaving you on this note:

Look around you. This is a place that is considered to be sacred. As each of you entered here, you felt that this place would do something for you or was giving something to you and that you could become something greater, fuller because of what you have received here. You began to feel the holiness here and therefore in yourselves.

You became reverent as soon as you walked through that gate. Many of you began to have spiritual experiences and felt your hearts expanding. I could feel you feeling the depths of your experiences.

But it isn't about this place. It is about you. Life is sacred. *You* are sacred.

What you are feeling is coming from within you. It is based upon your perceptions, your emotions, your hopes, wishes, and dreams. And you are only allowing yourselves to feel this in a place that you feel is appropriate or safe.

Let yourselves feel this in every moment of life. Feel deeply. Live fully.

I have a question for you. Don't answer it for me, or for us, just answer it for you.

The ancients left this place for people to come to for eons after they were here. They knew the importance of tradition and ritual, of what is sacred. What will you leave upon this earth when you are gone? What have you given in return for what you have received? Or are you all just taking what you can, while you can?

At this point, there was an audible gasp as the recognition of my words sank in. I was hitting home. Perfect. I continued:

Know that for every action there is a reaction, a rippling outward of consequences that continue on infinitely.

Know that every action you take, every word you speak, every thought you have, any energy of any kind that you expend affects the entirety. And you are affected by all that happens within the entirety. This is a mutual exchange that happens on the most minute and grandest levels of being.

Live intentionally. Know that you are always holy and whatever you choose in any given moment is the most perfect decision you could have ever made simply because you made it.

That you have the free will to determine the outcome of any situation in your life is a gift from the heavens that will never wear out.

Receiving and taking are two completely different animals. To take denotes possession. To receive denotes a gift. Let everything that you experience be a gift. Receive gracefully and with gratitude, and always, always be willing to do your part. You have to pray and move your feet.

And remember that all of your actions in all of your life leave an indelible mark upon this world and beyond.

To this I would only add: That indelible mark, everything that you create now, will be lived through our children and your children's children and their children and their children's children.

We have the power to change the world today, as well as our future world, through the actions and patterns, beliefs and perceptions that we hand down as our legacy. A life well lived makes us immortal. What we do, what we have done, will touch others in ways we cannot imagine. When we change ourselves, having the lives we want, knowing that all actions must be intentional because every one has a definite effect—we get what we create and we leave that for all others in our succession.

We must be vigilant.

First with ourselves.

Then all others.

As we are, we exercise the very power of the infinite right here on earth and fuel it for all time.

About the Author

Meg Blackburn Losey, PhD, is the host of the Internet radio show "Cosmic Particles." She is the author of *Touching the Light, The Secret History of Consciousness, The Children of Now,* and *The Living Light Cards.* She is also a contributor to the anthology *The Mystery of 2012: Predictions, Prophecies, and Possibilities.*

Dr. Meg is the creator of the Touching the Light Healing Modality and offers certification courses. Information is available at *touchingthelight.org.*

Dr. Meg is a national and international Keynote Speaker and lectures worldwide. She facilitates group journeys to sacred sites in Scotland, England, Ireland, Peru, Bolivia, Egypt, and Mexico. She has also served as a consultant to Good Morning America and 20/20. Dr. Meg can be reached by email at drmeg@spiritlite.com, or via her website at *www.spiritlite.com.* She is also available via LinkedIn, Facebook, and Twitter as DocSpirit.

To Our Readers

Weiser Books, an imprint of Red Wheel/Weiser, publishes books across the entire spectrum of occult, esoteric, speculative, and New Age subjects. Our mission is to publish quality books that will make a difference in people's lives without advocating any one particular path or field of study. We value the integrity, originality, and depth of knowledge of our authors.

Our readers are our most important resource, and we appreciate your input, suggestions, and ideas about what you would like to see published.

Visit our website at *www.redwheelweiser.com* to learn about our upcoming books and free downloads, and be sure to go to *www.redwheelweiser.com/newsletter* to sign up for newsletters and exclusive offers.

You can also contact us at info@redwheelweiser.com or at

Red Wheel/Weiser, LLC
665 Third Street, Suite 400
San Francisco, CA 94107